PICTURE BOOK OF

RELAXING SEASONAL

...By...

Ella Caldwell

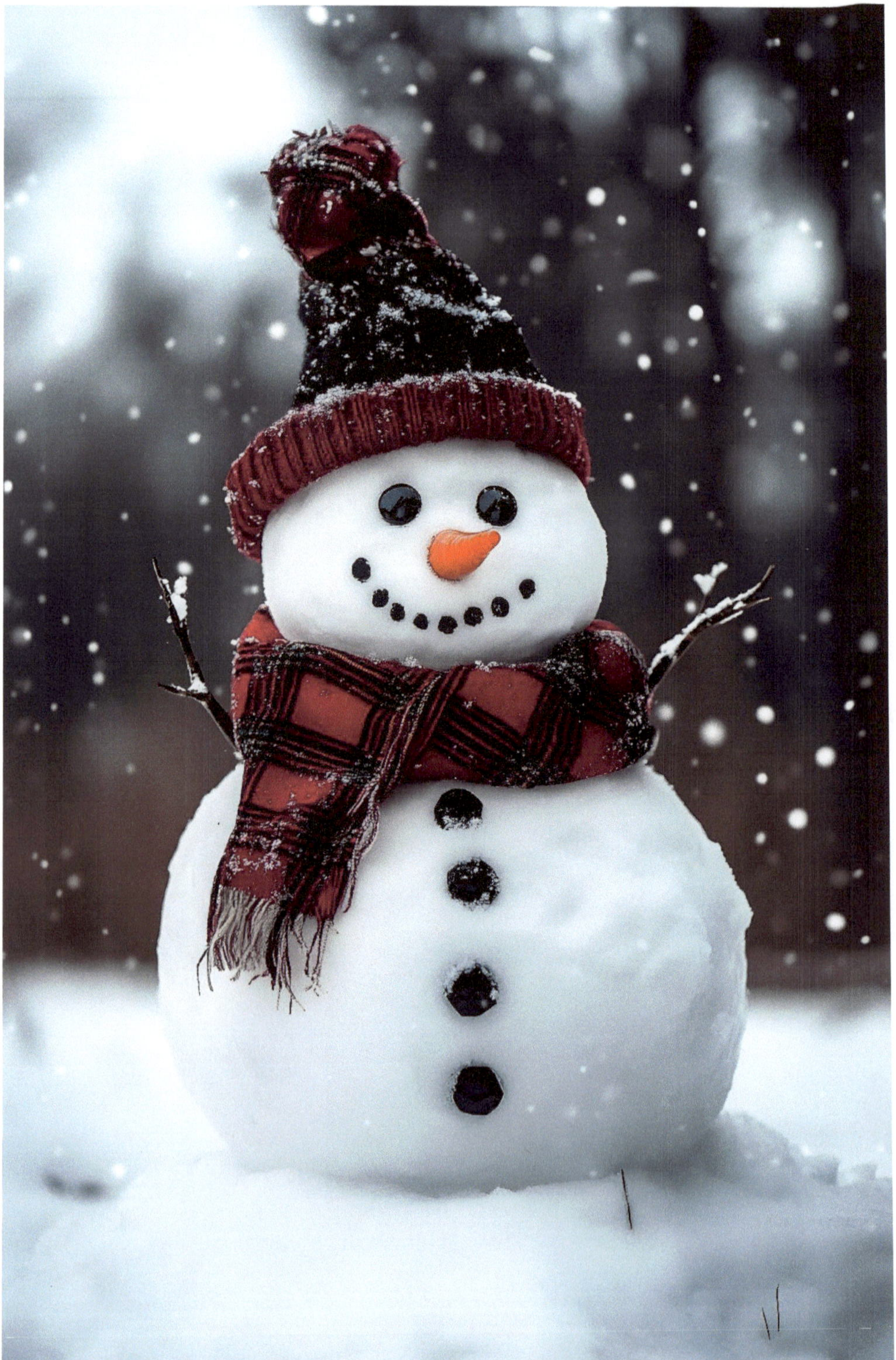

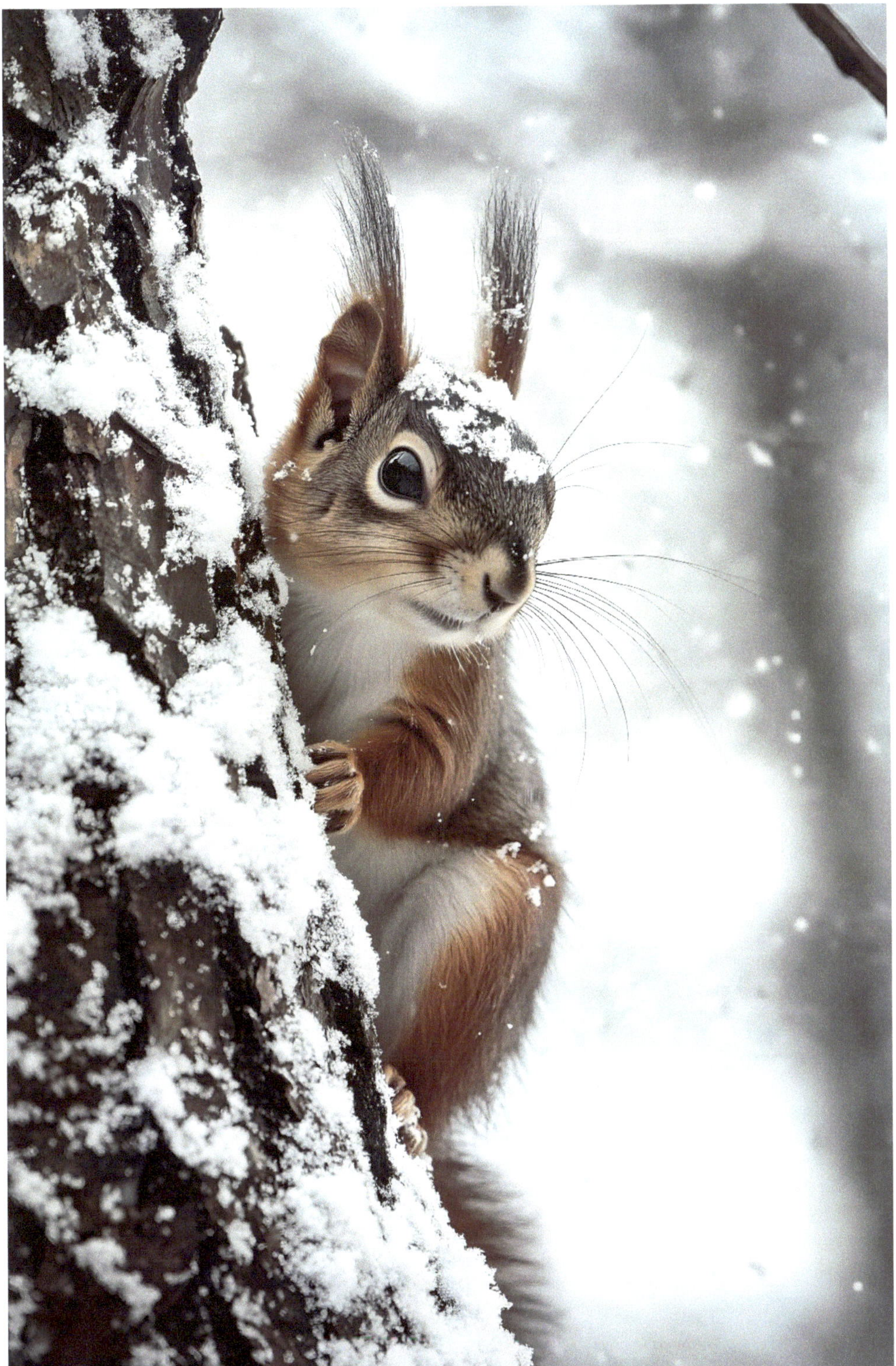

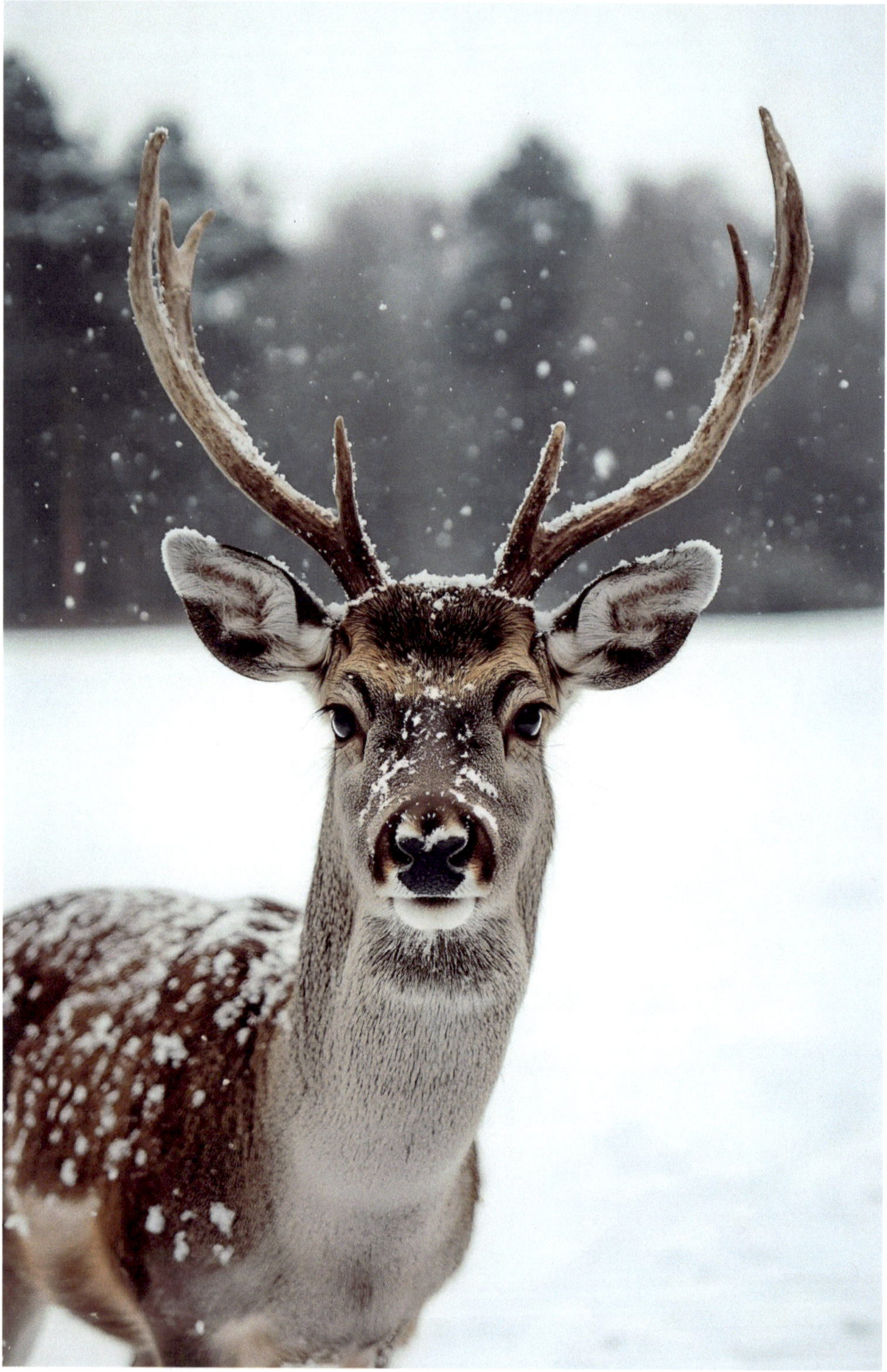

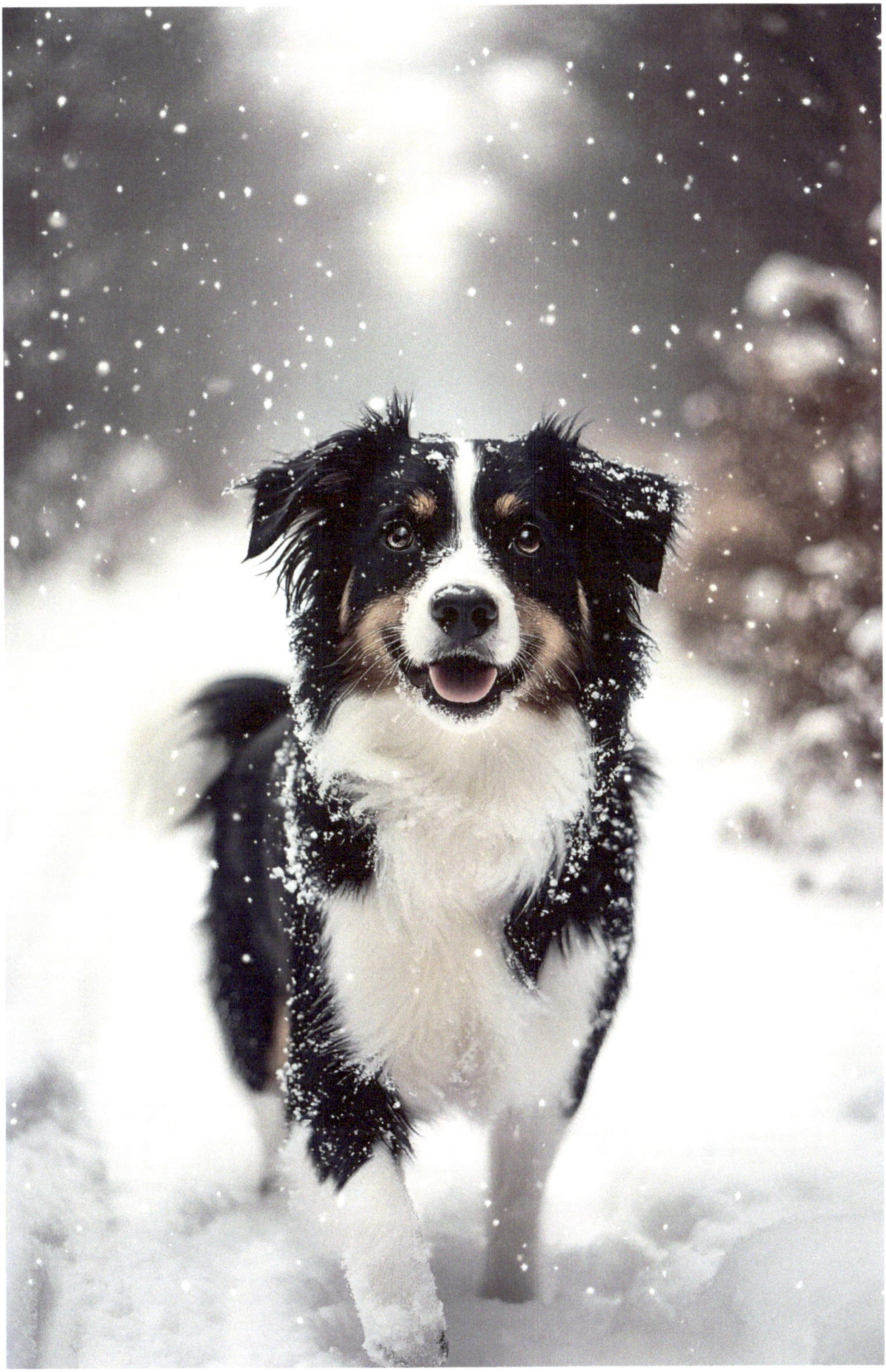

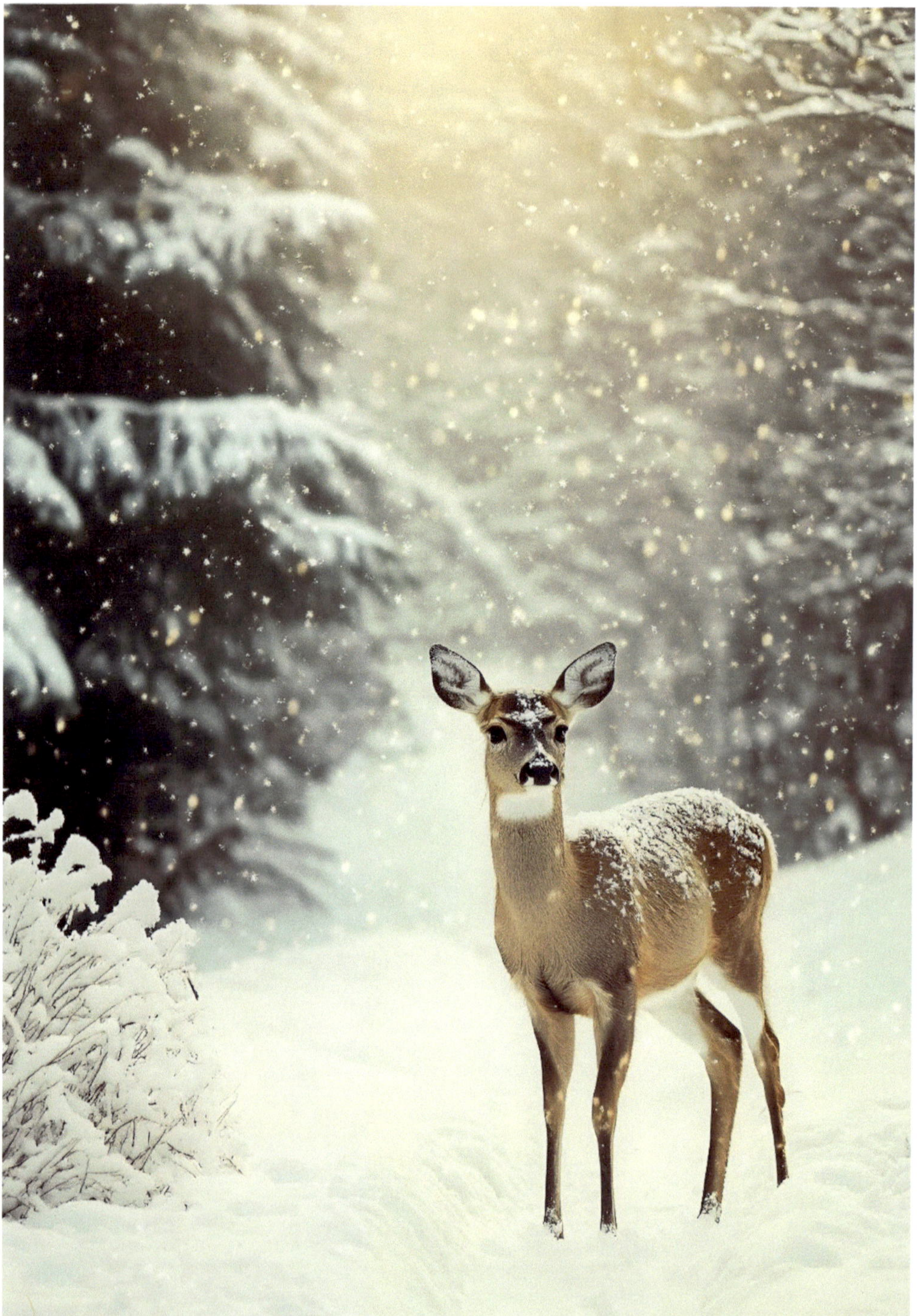

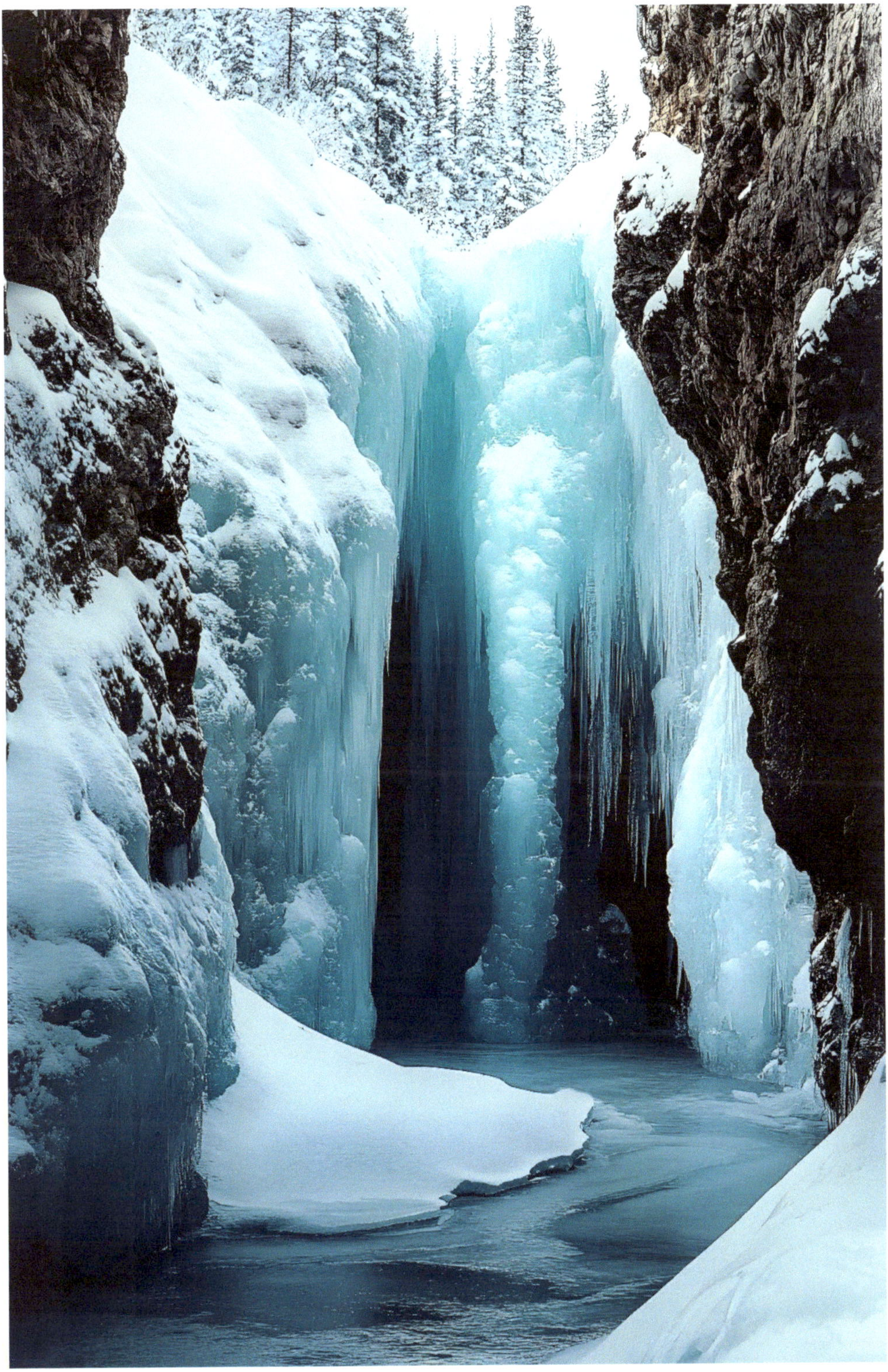

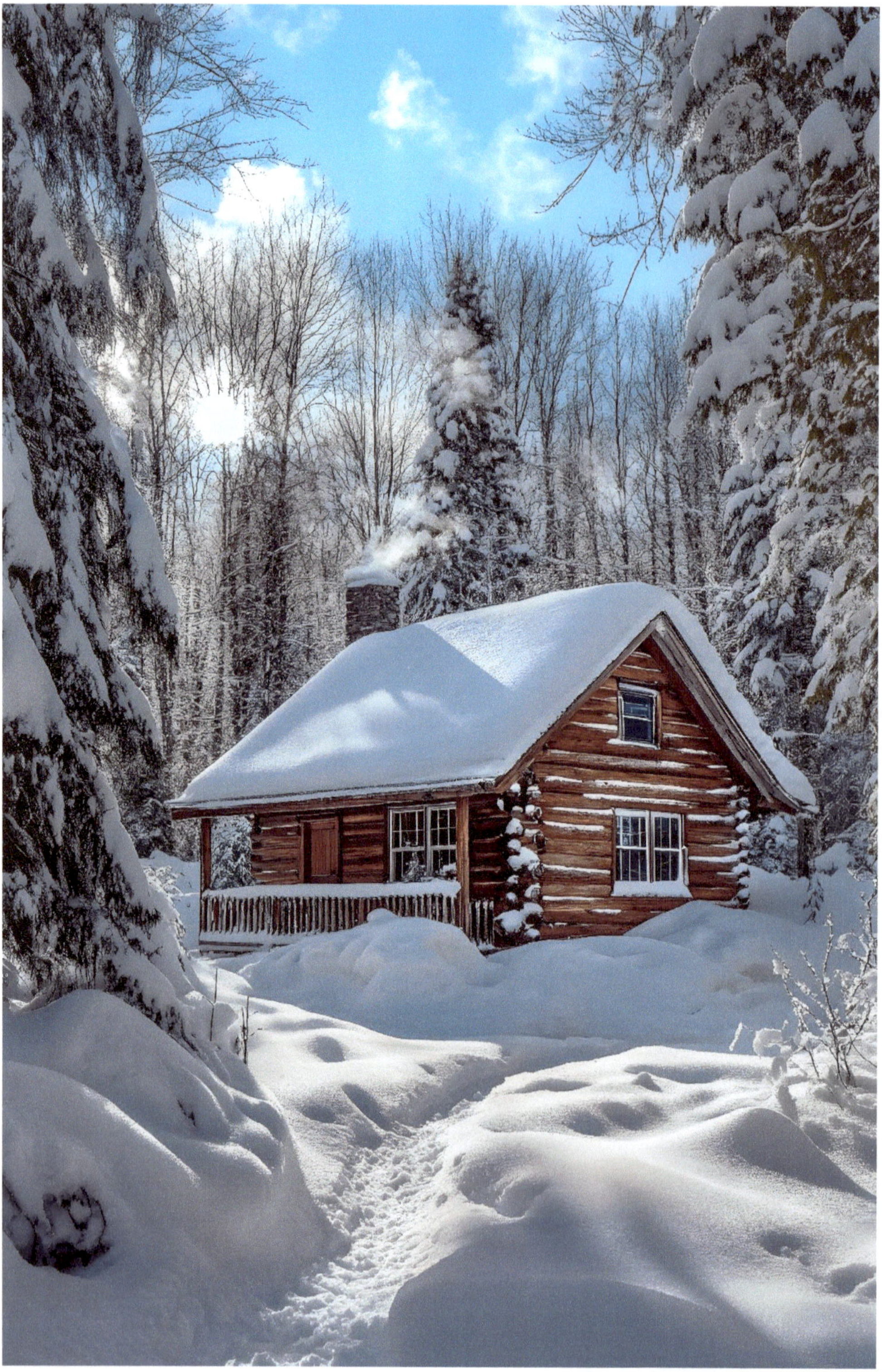

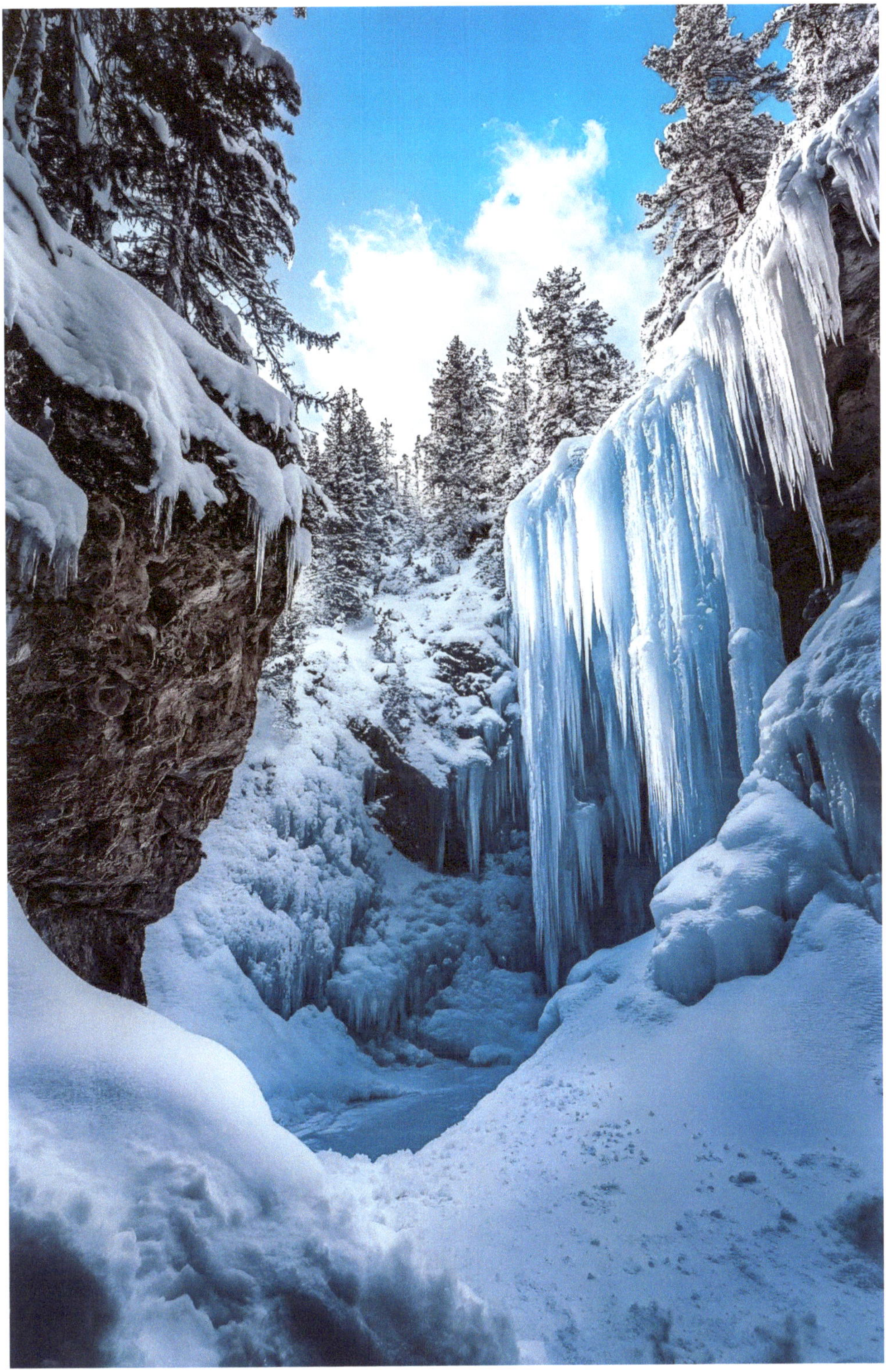

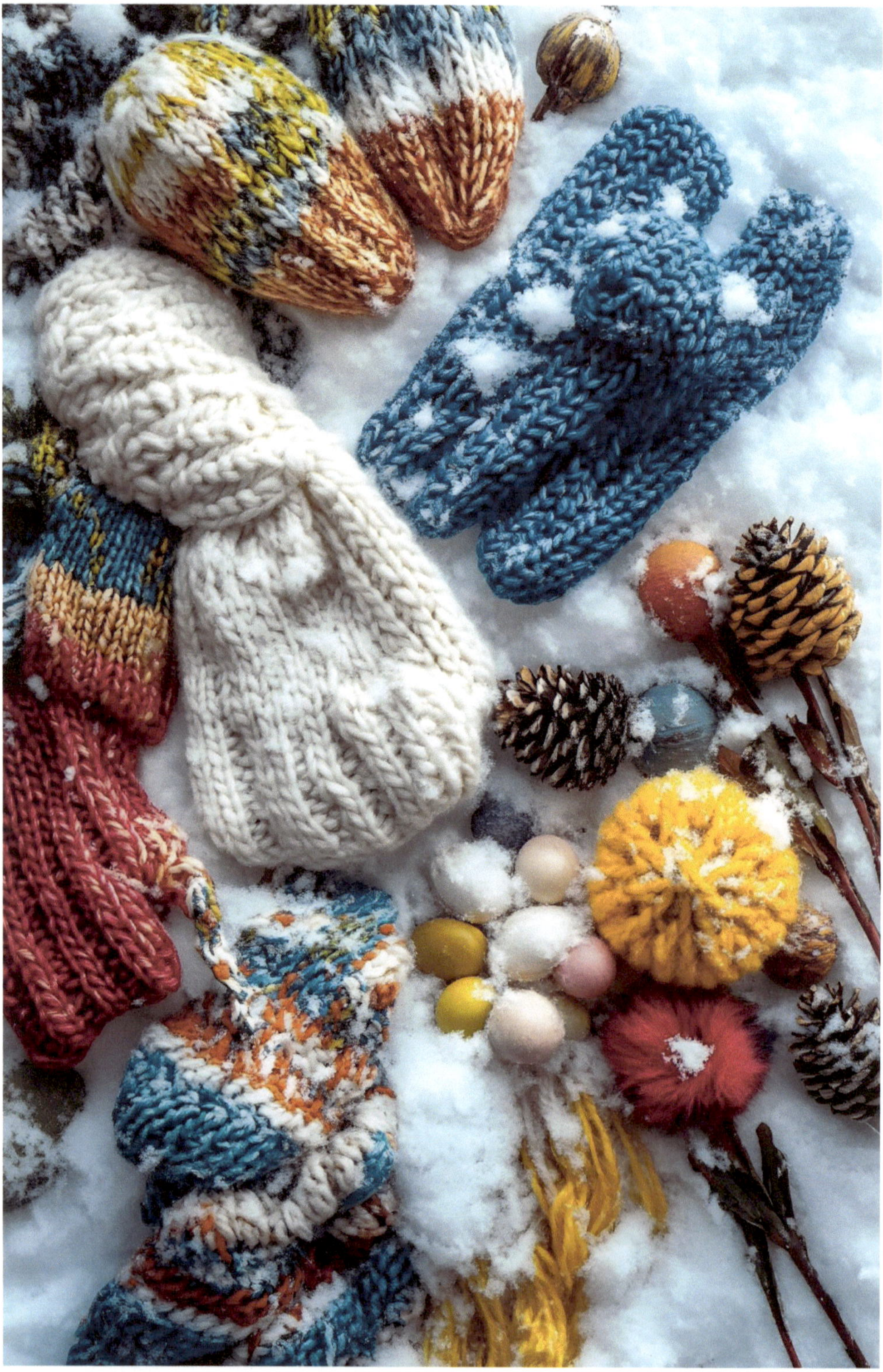

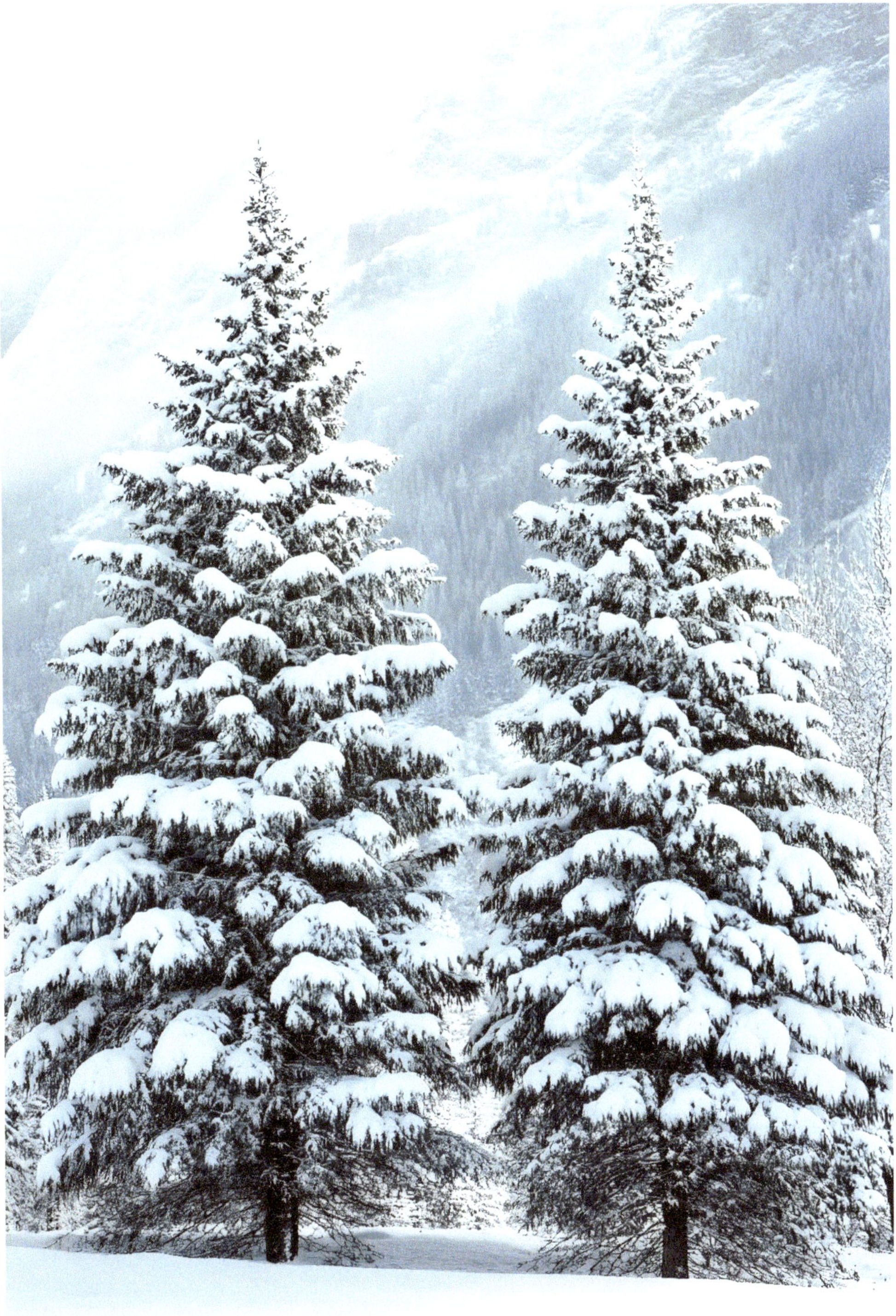

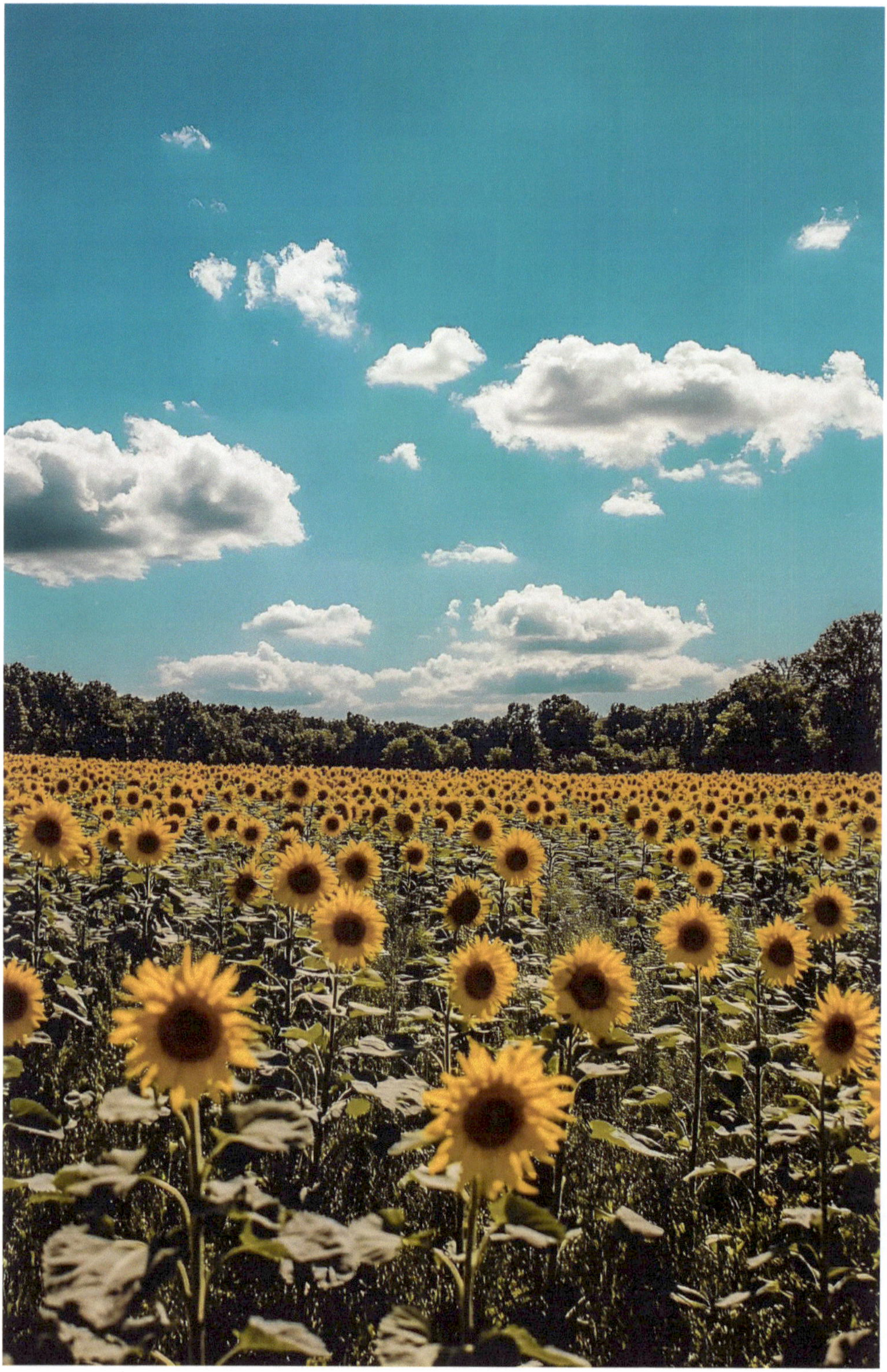

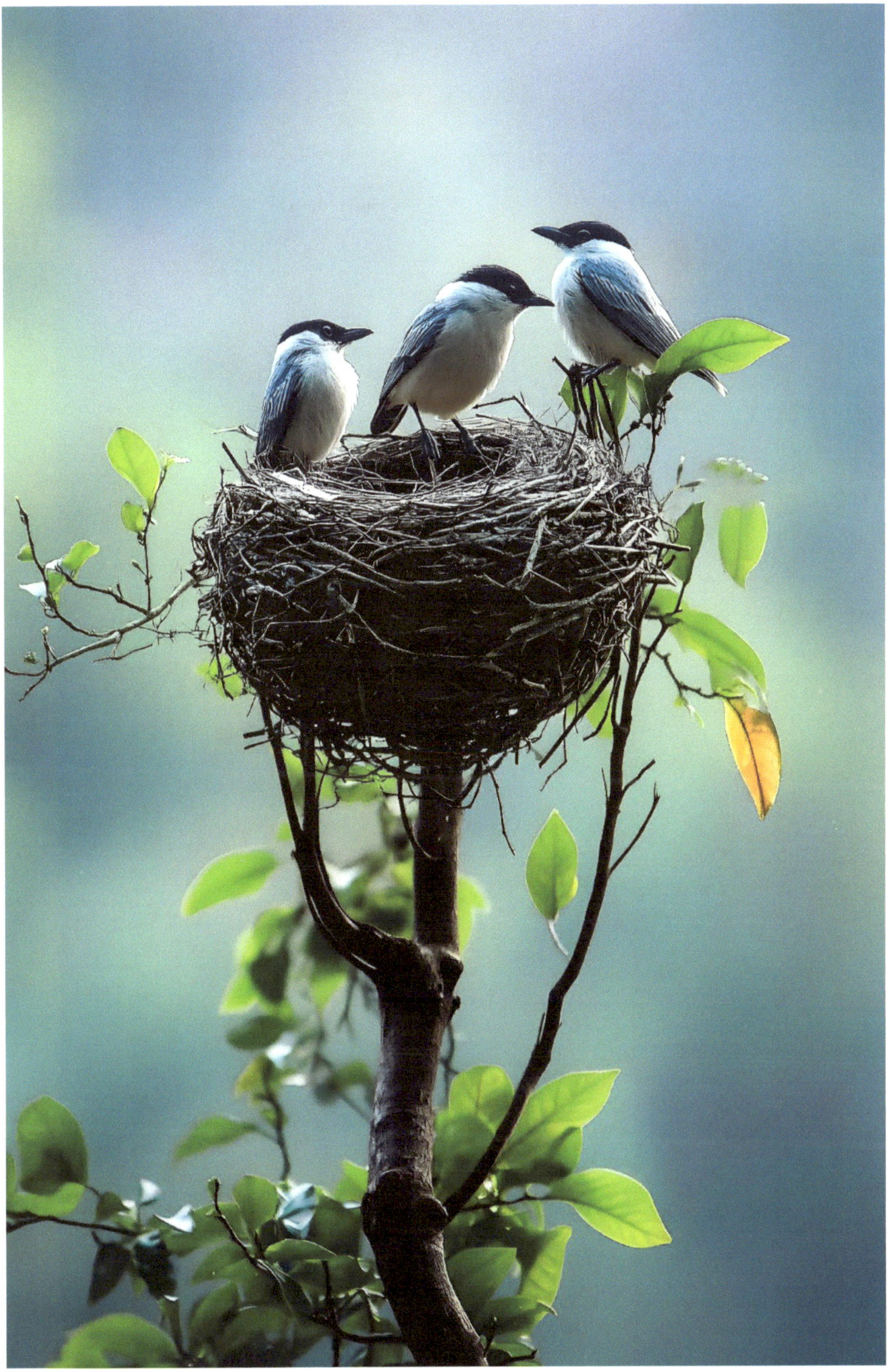

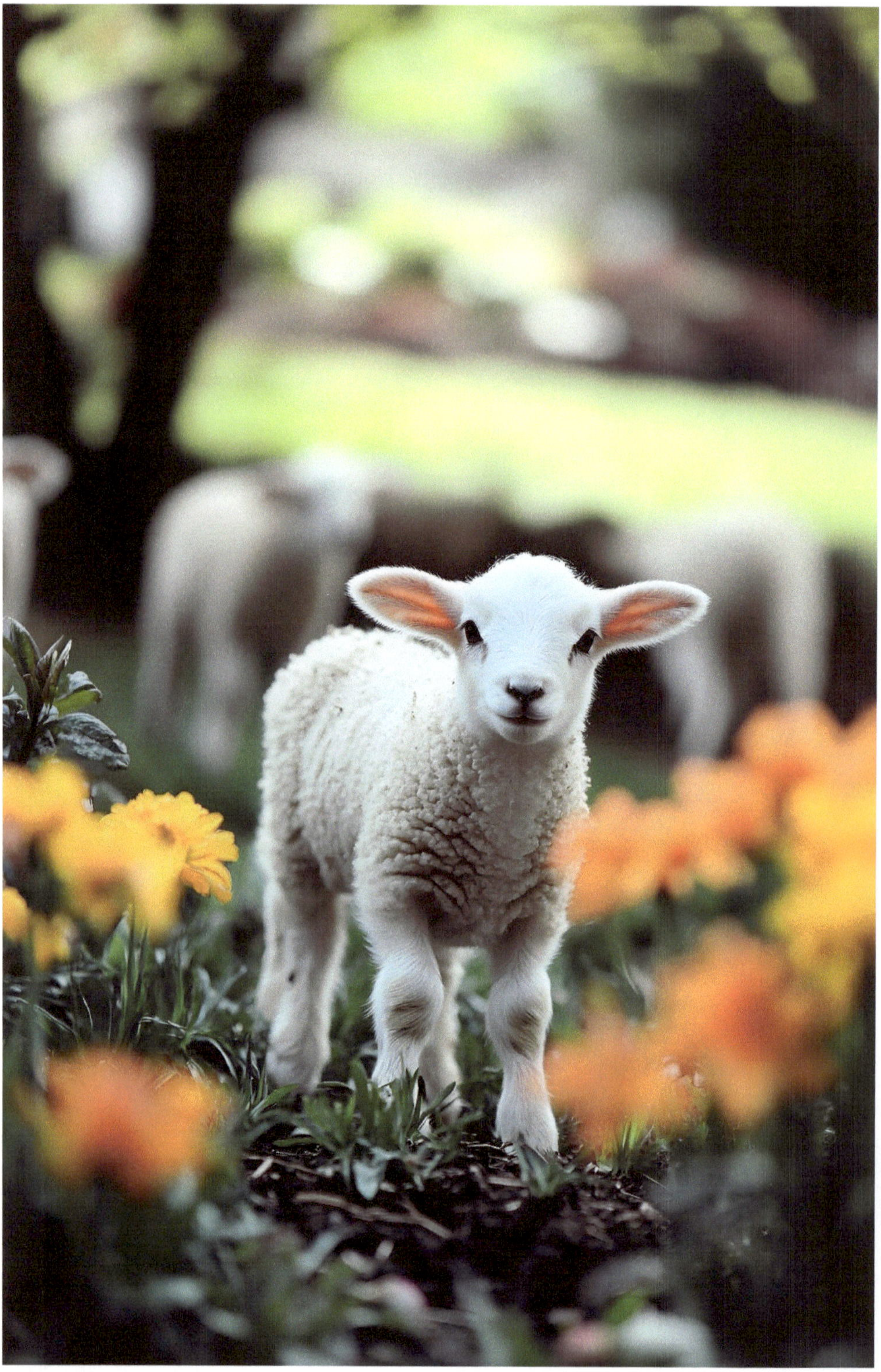

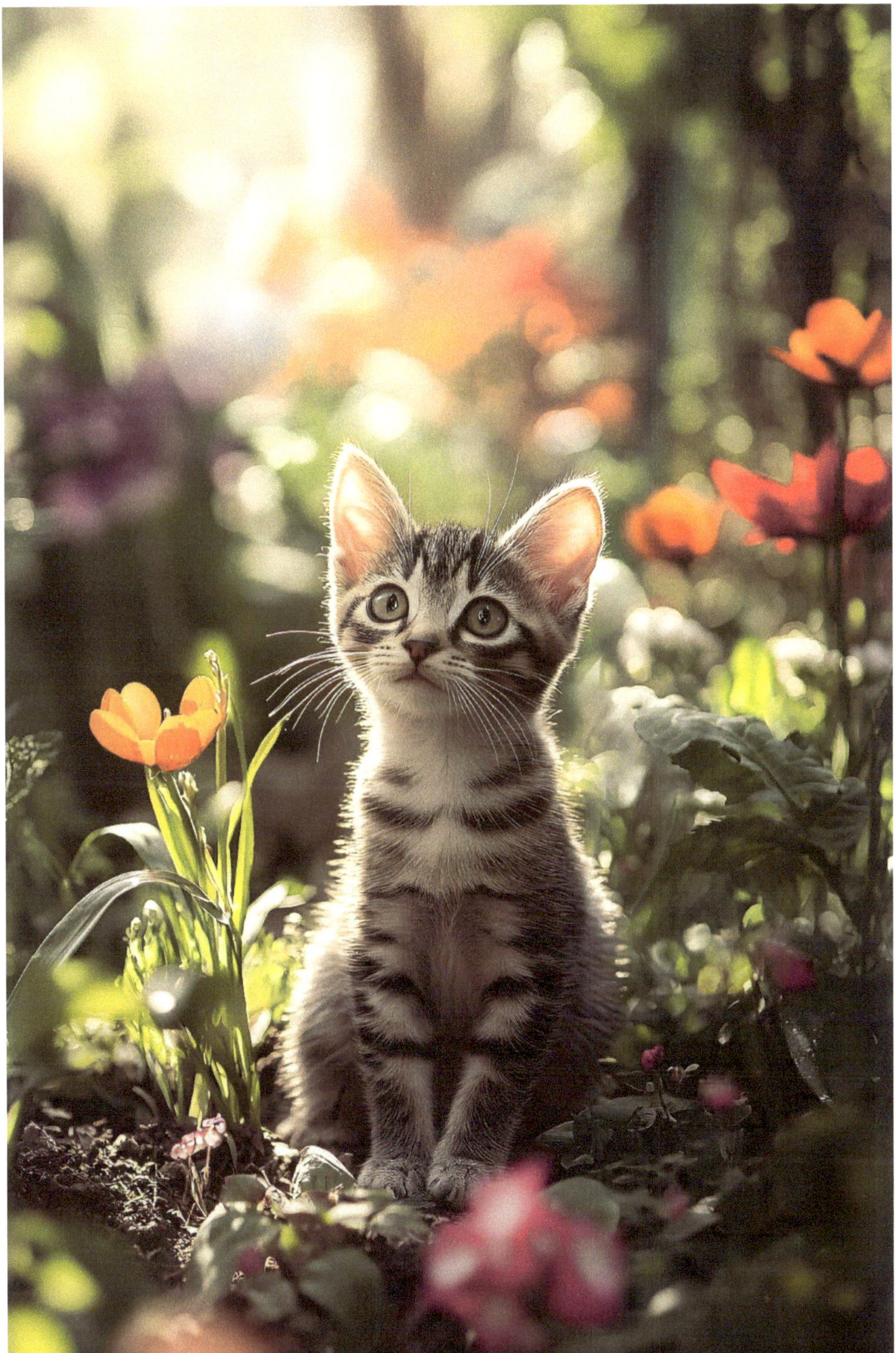

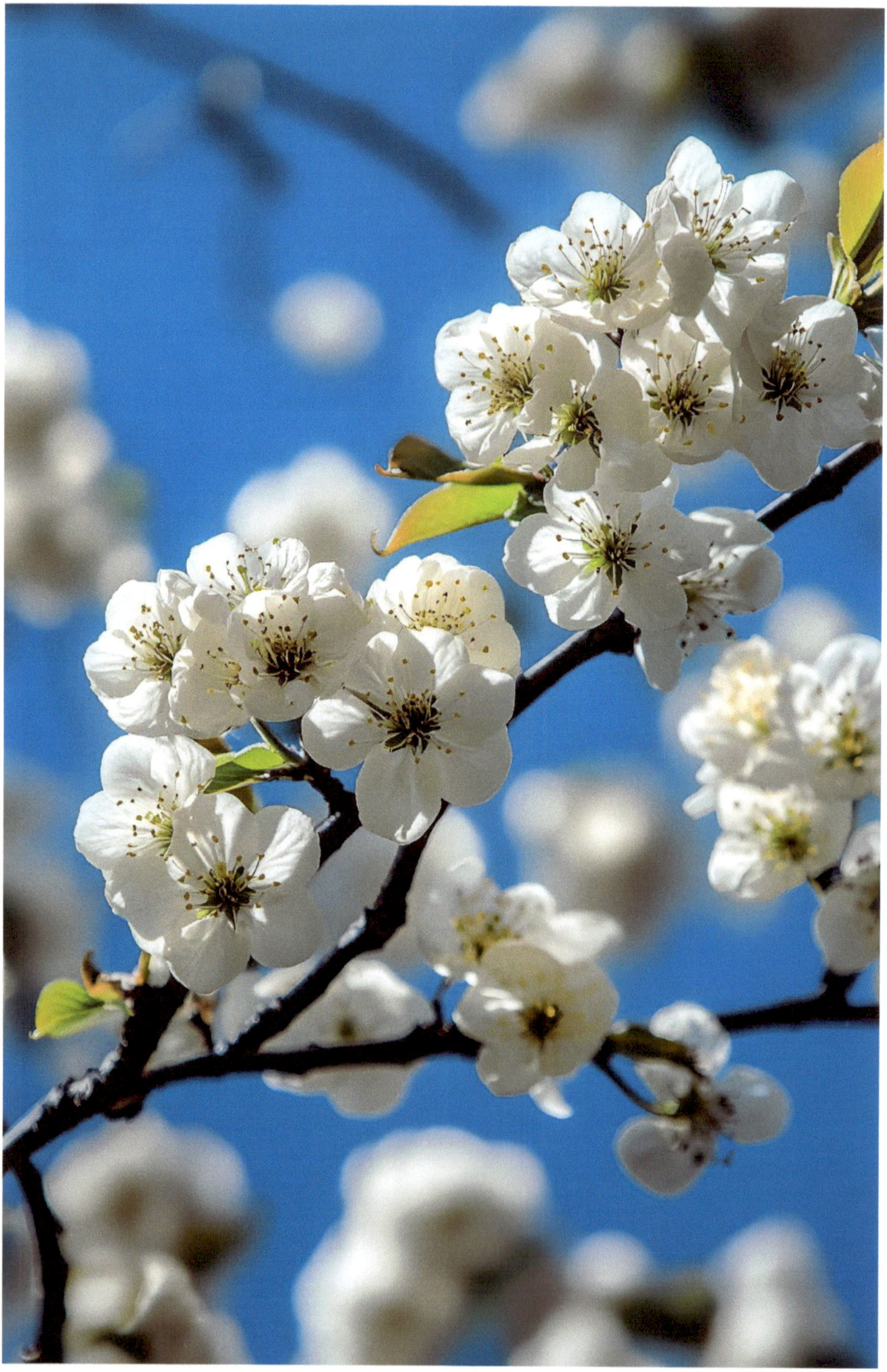

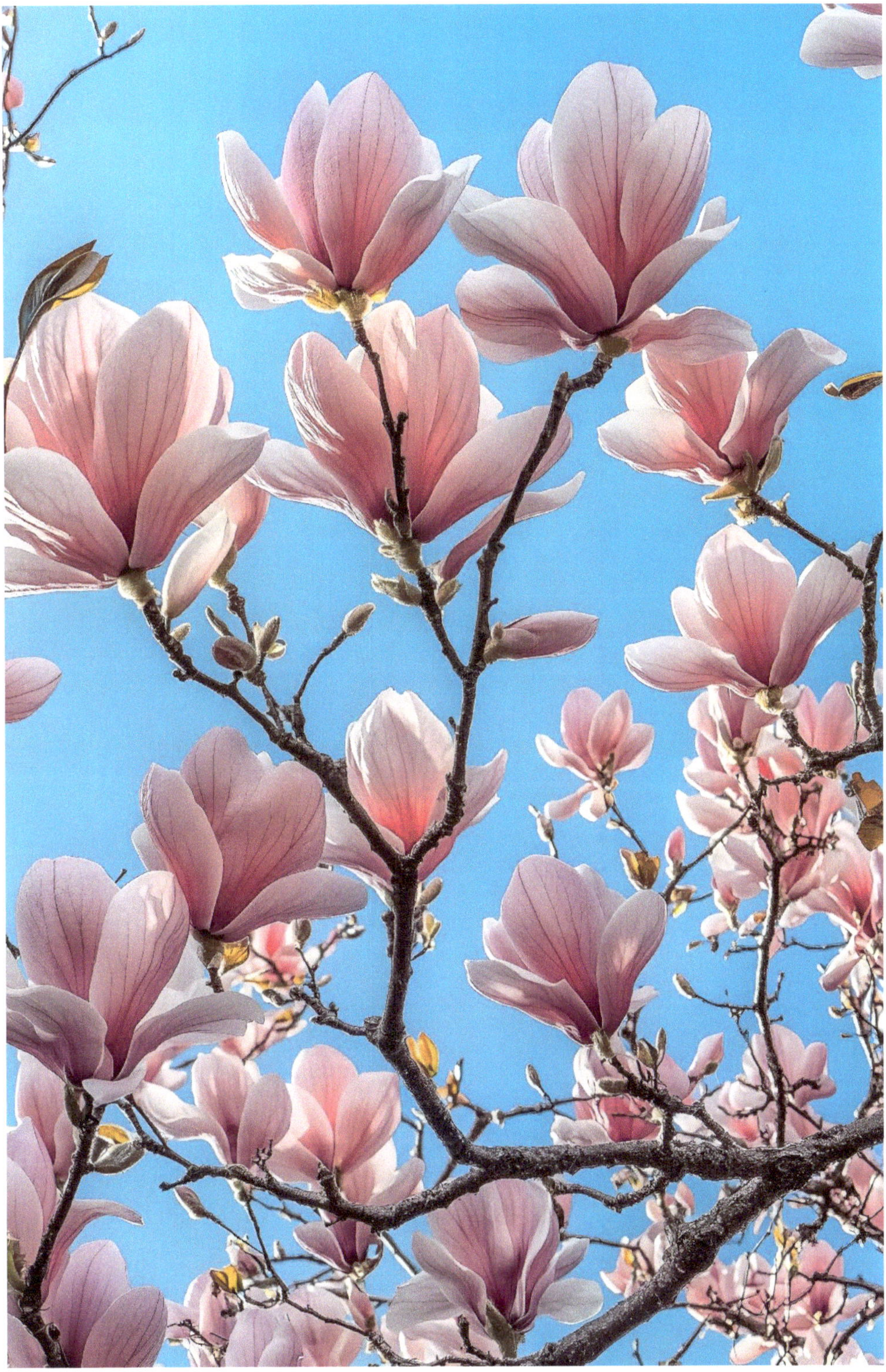

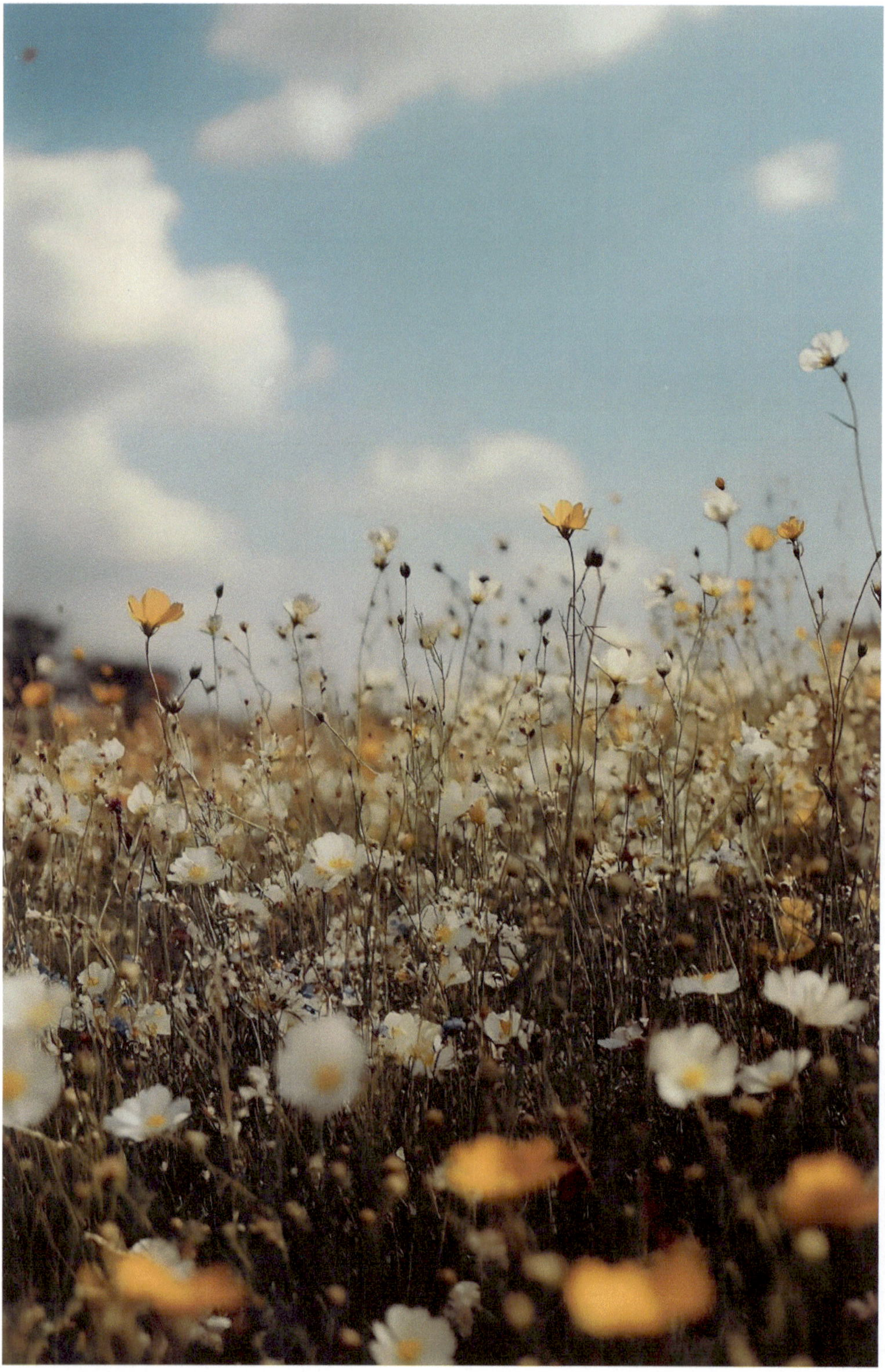

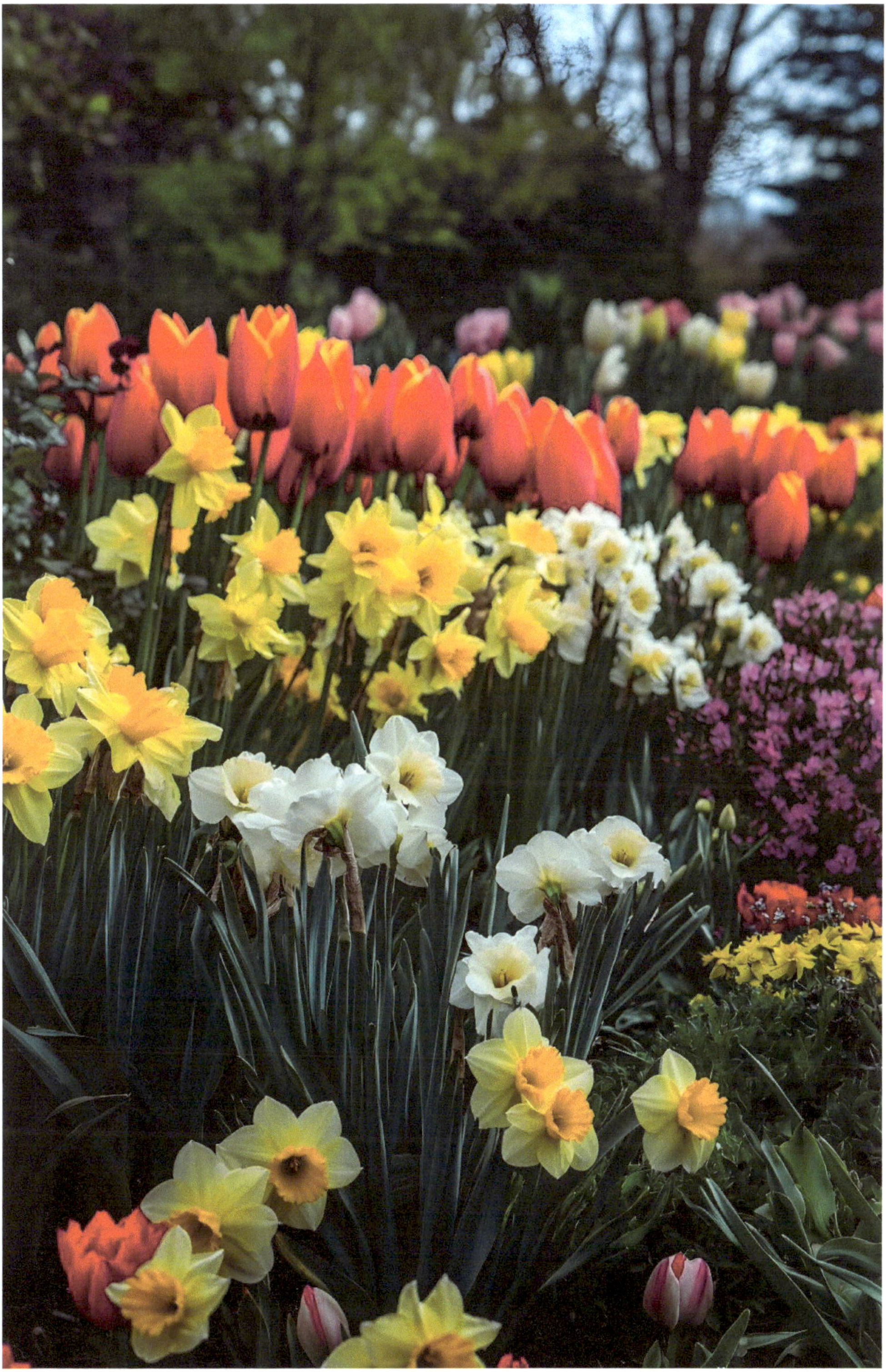

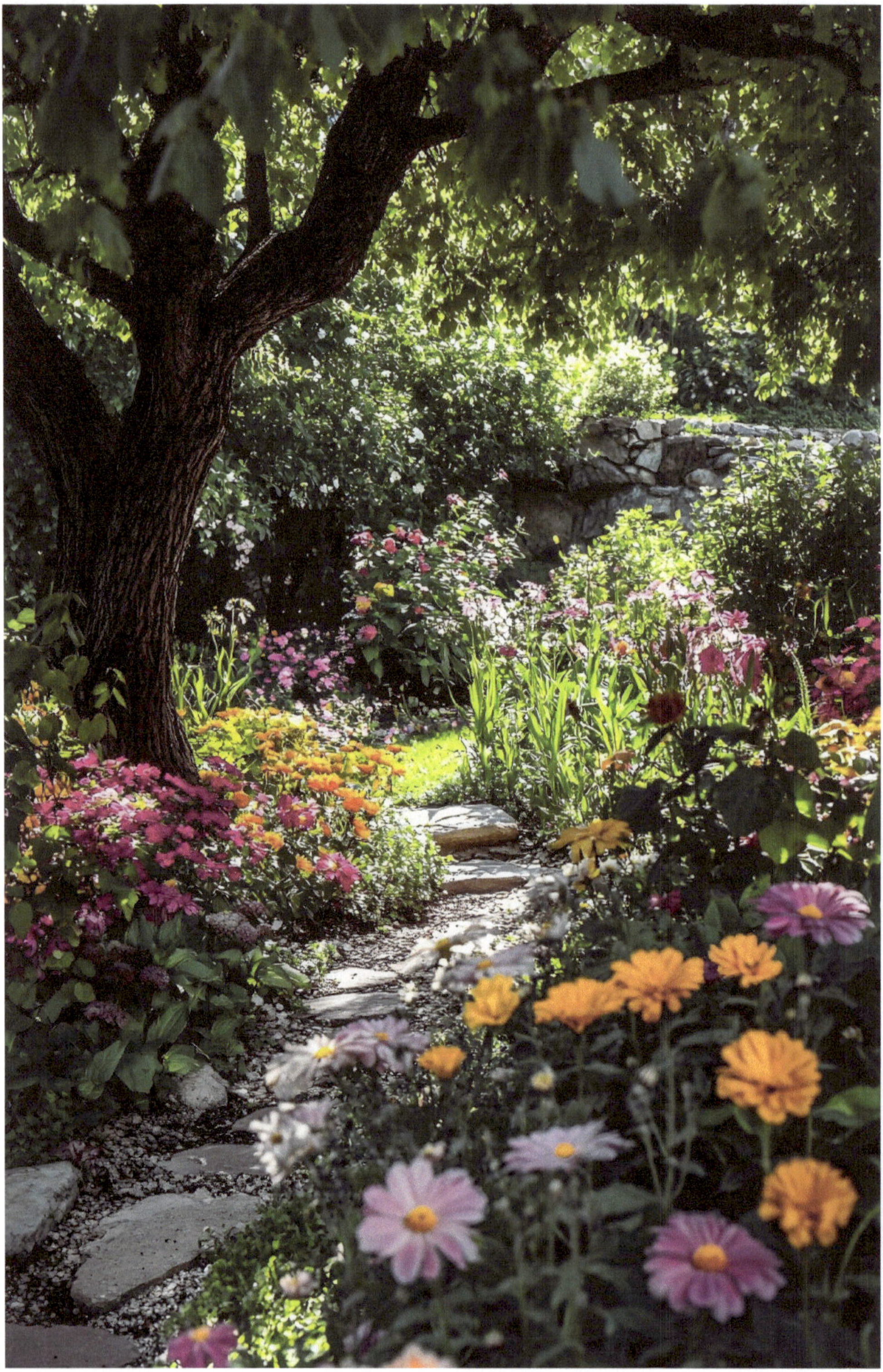

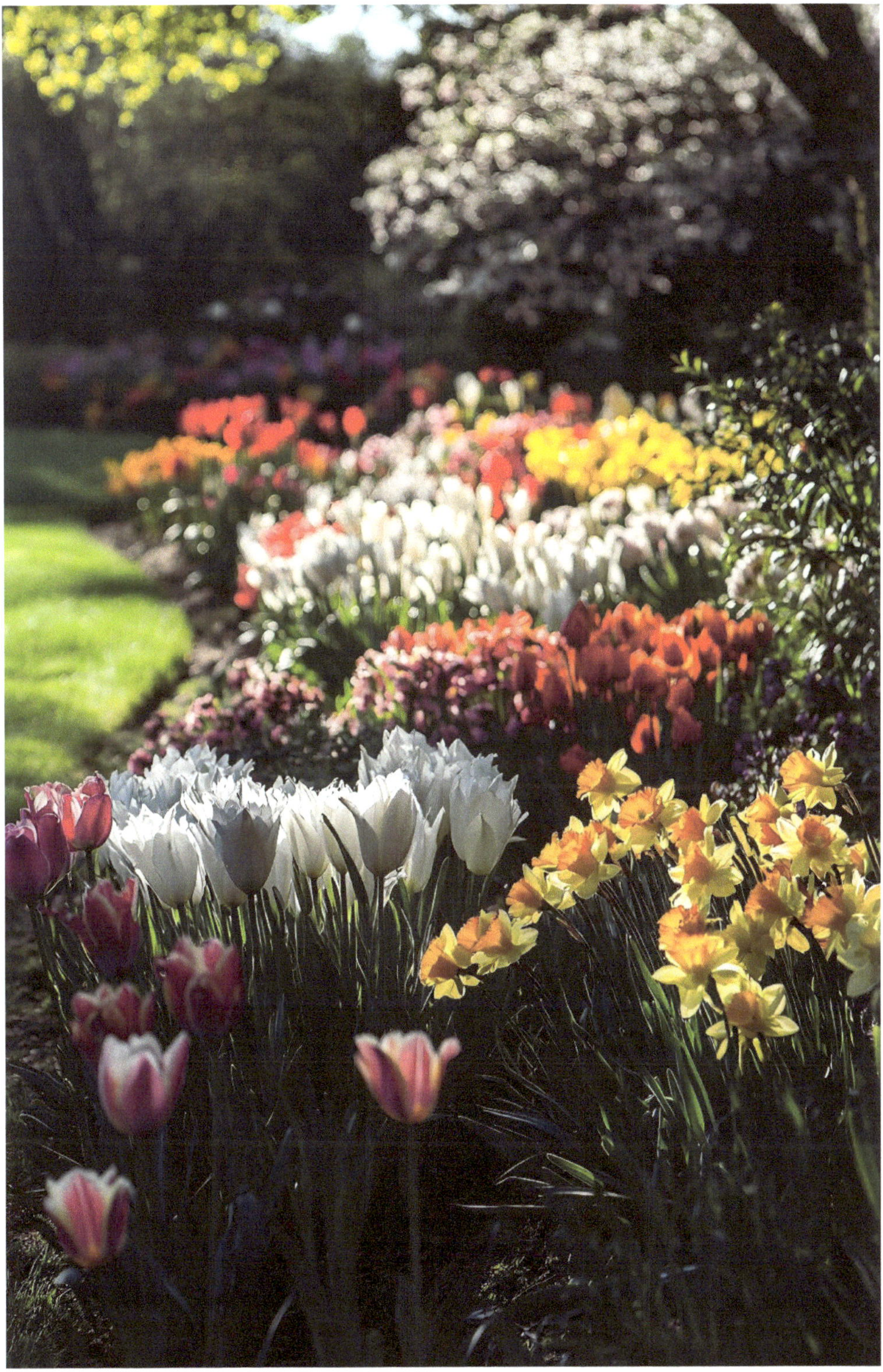

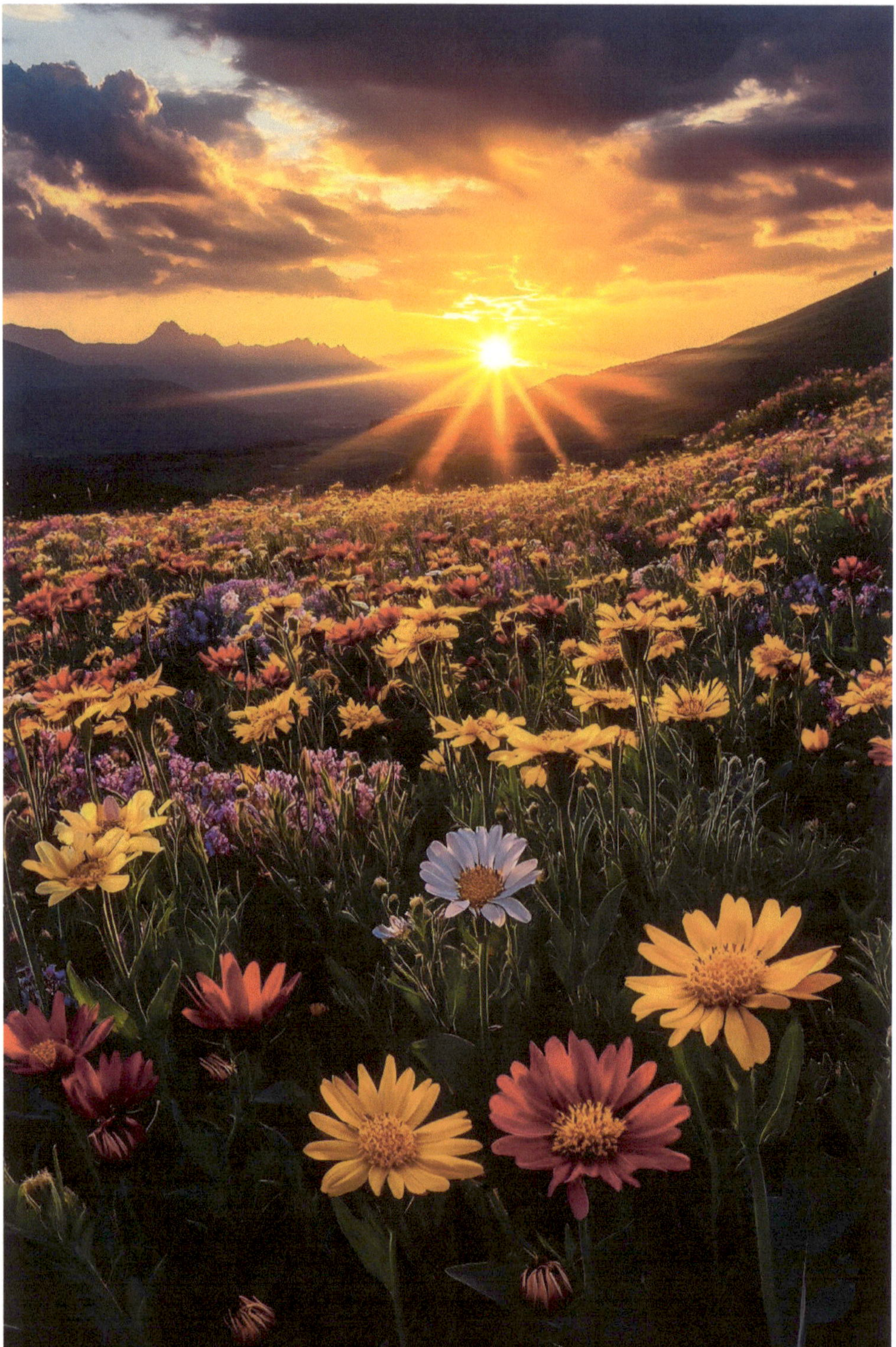

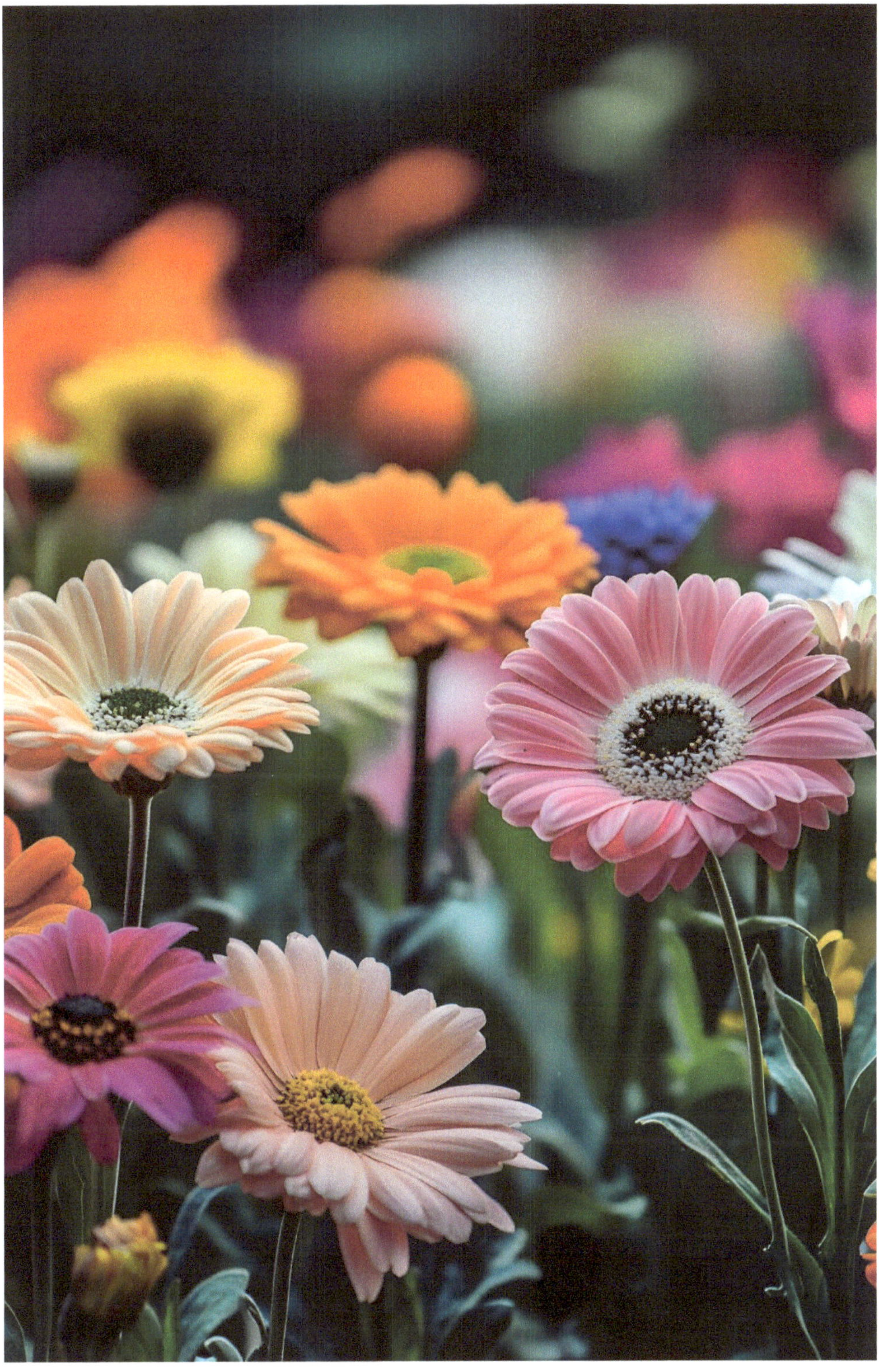

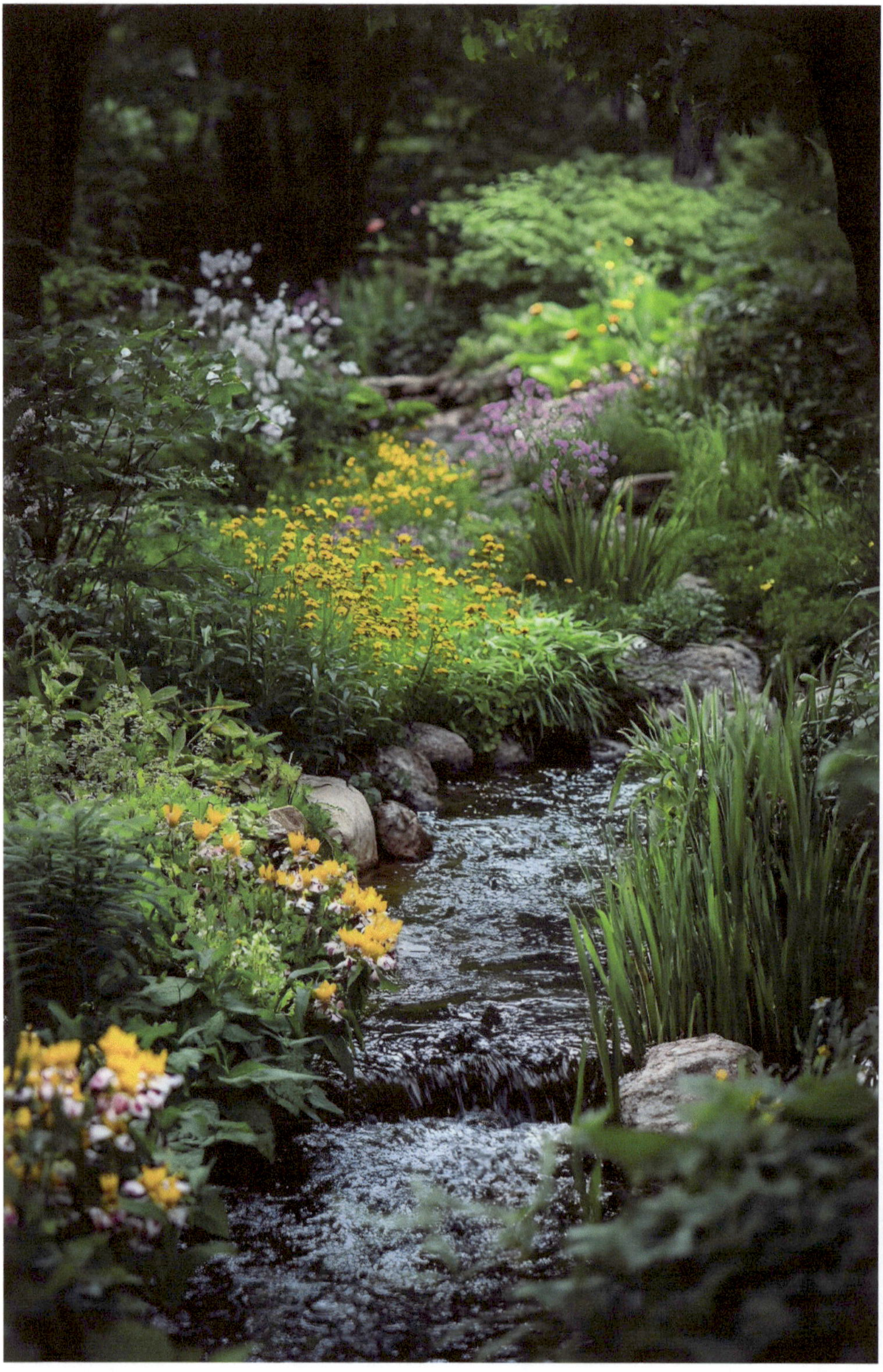

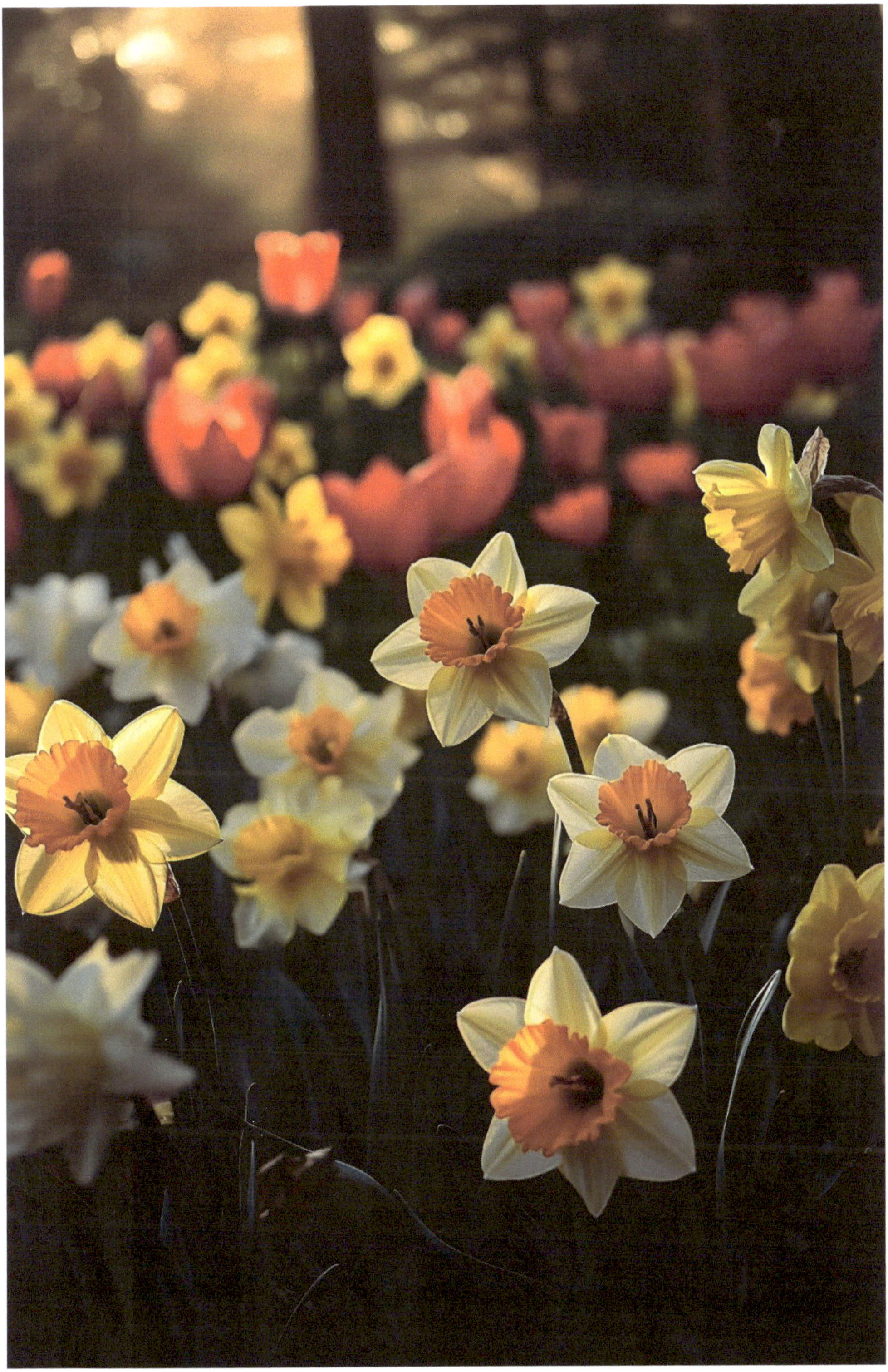

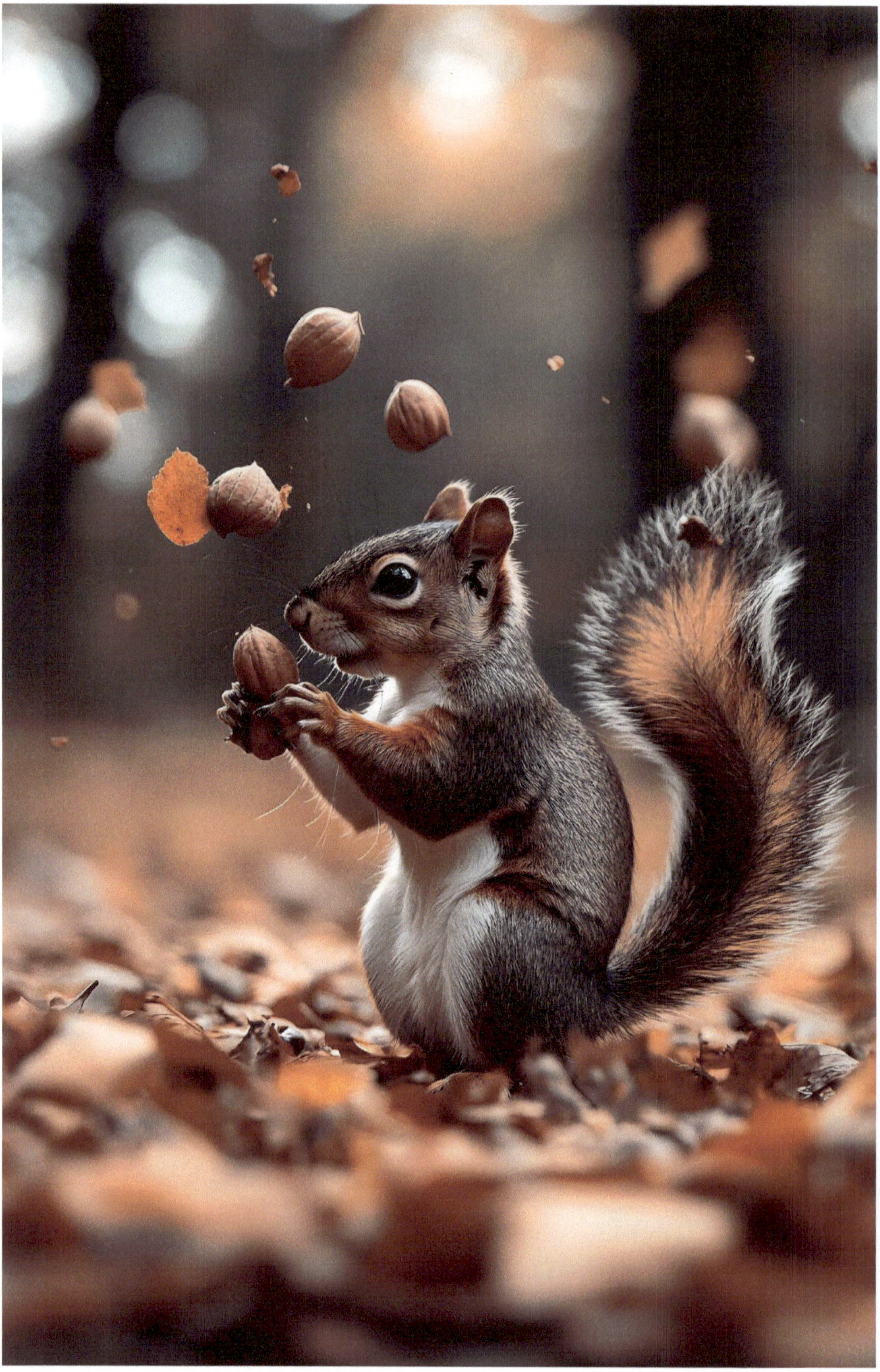

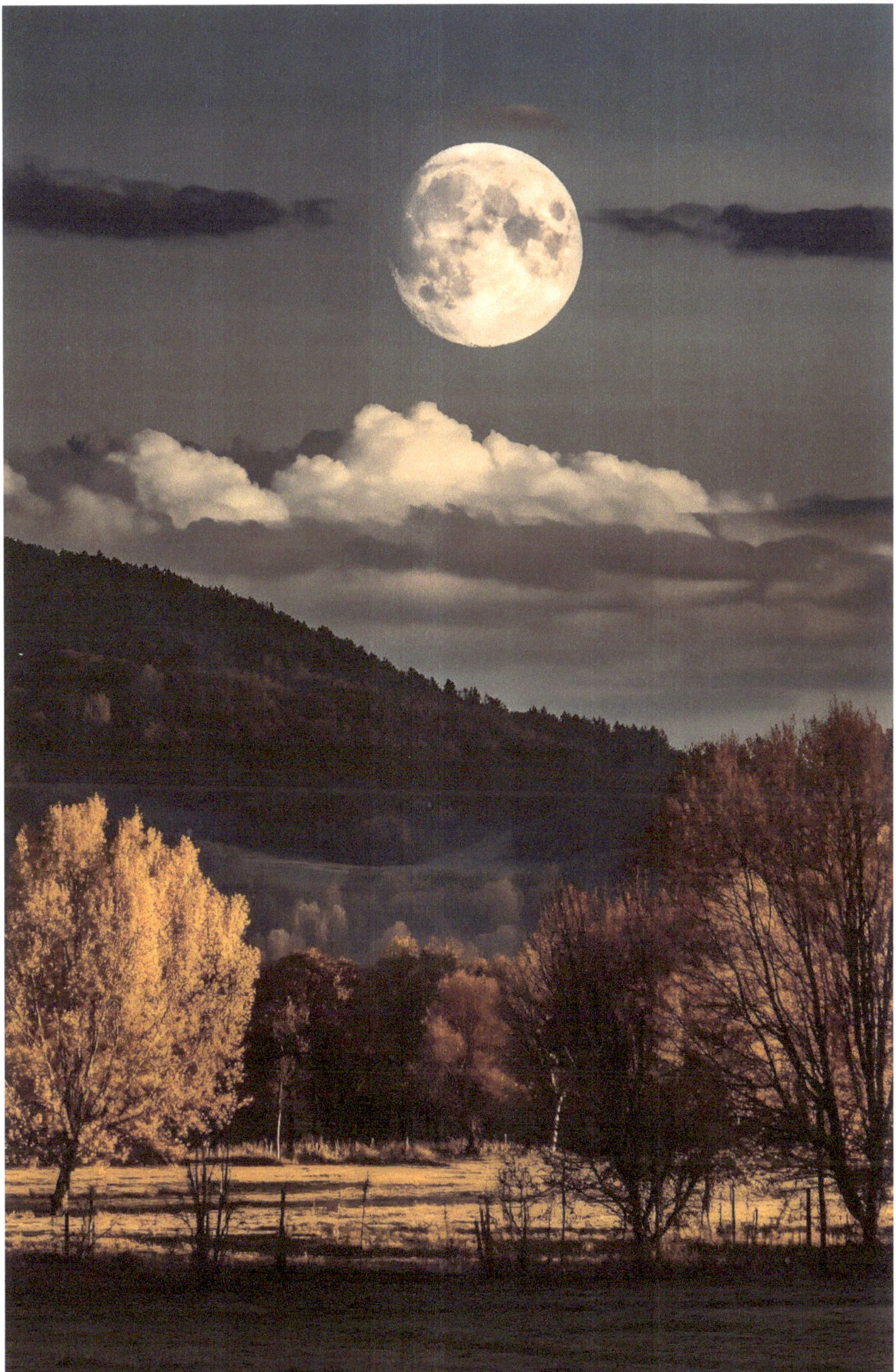

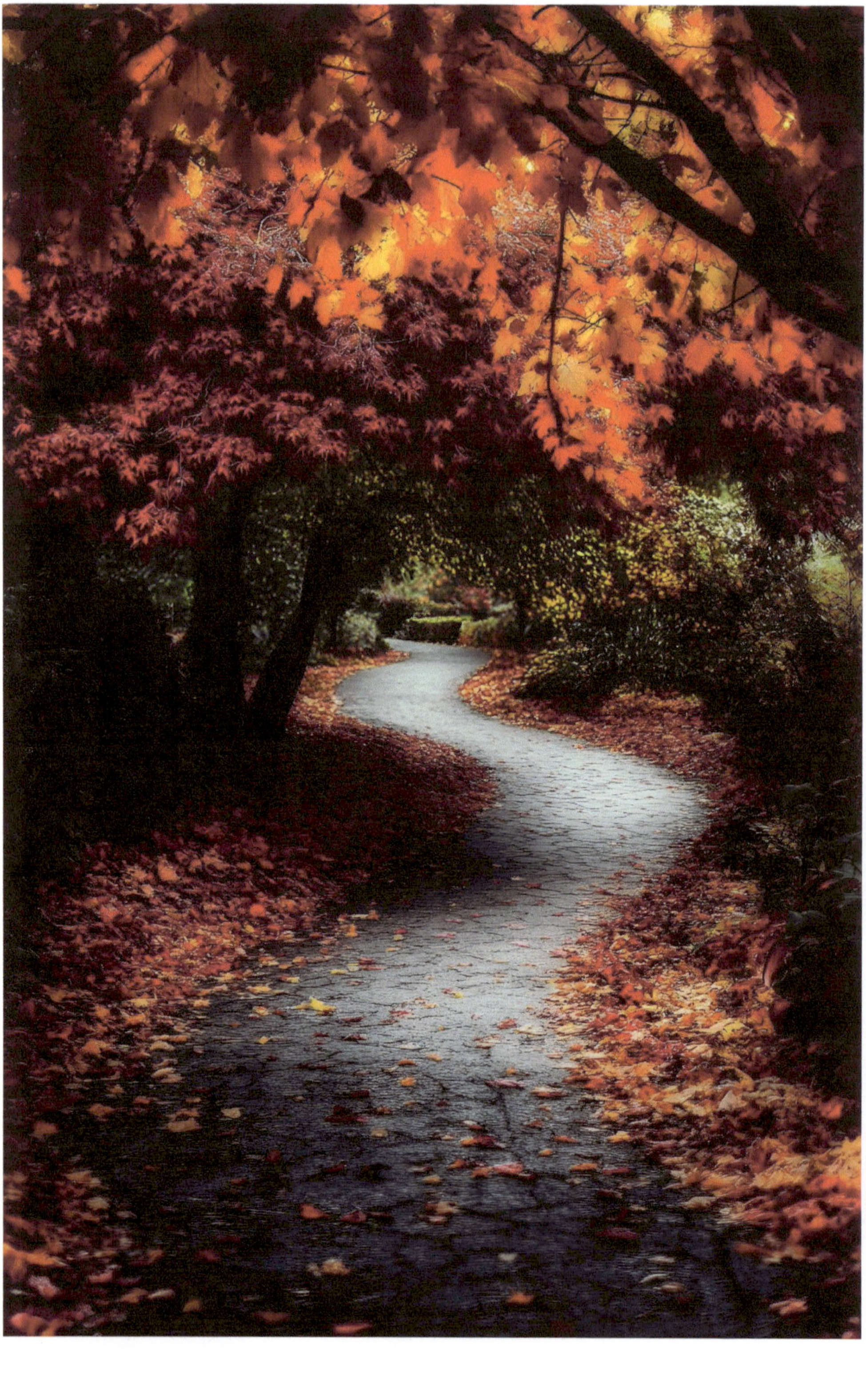

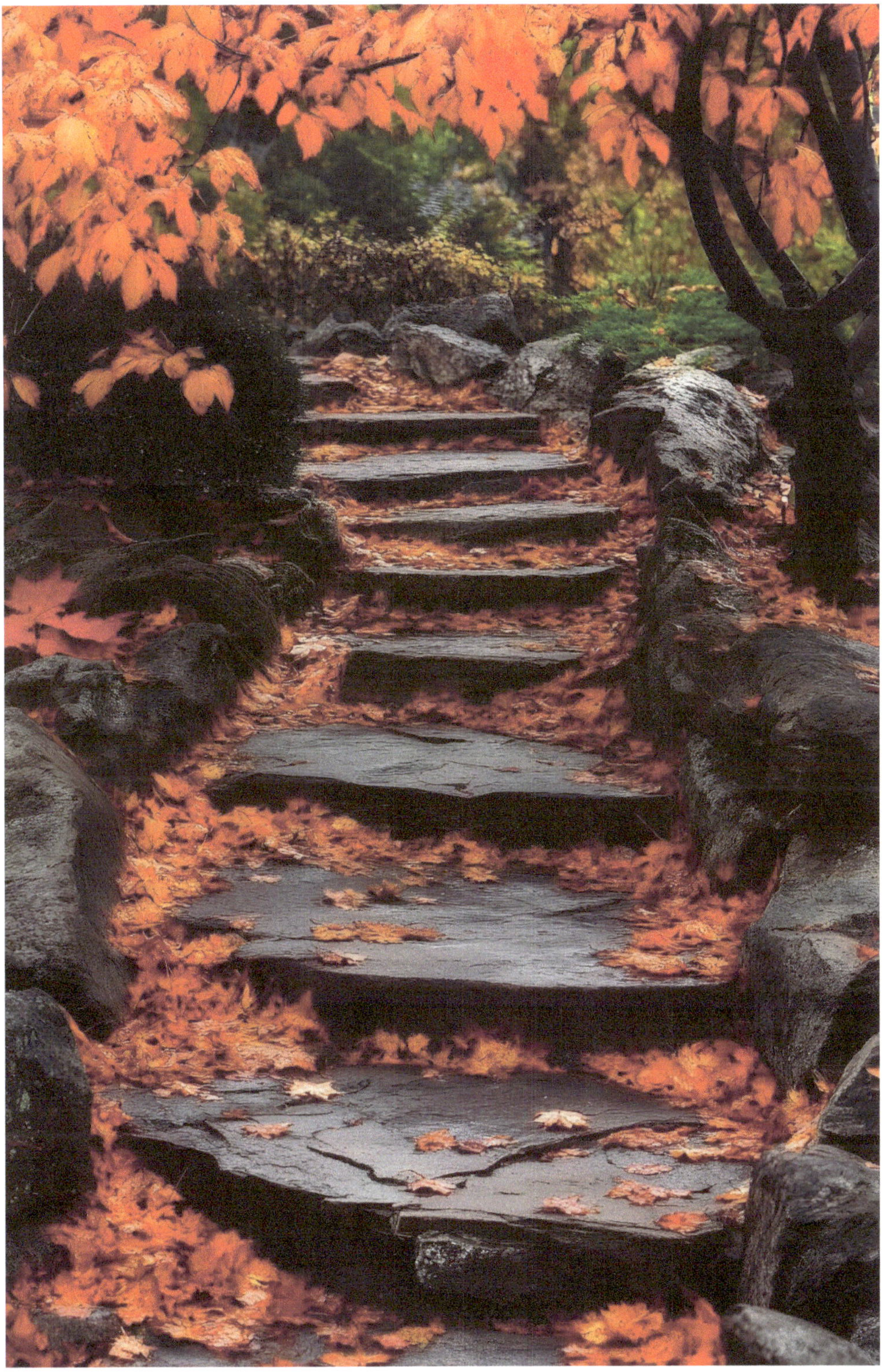

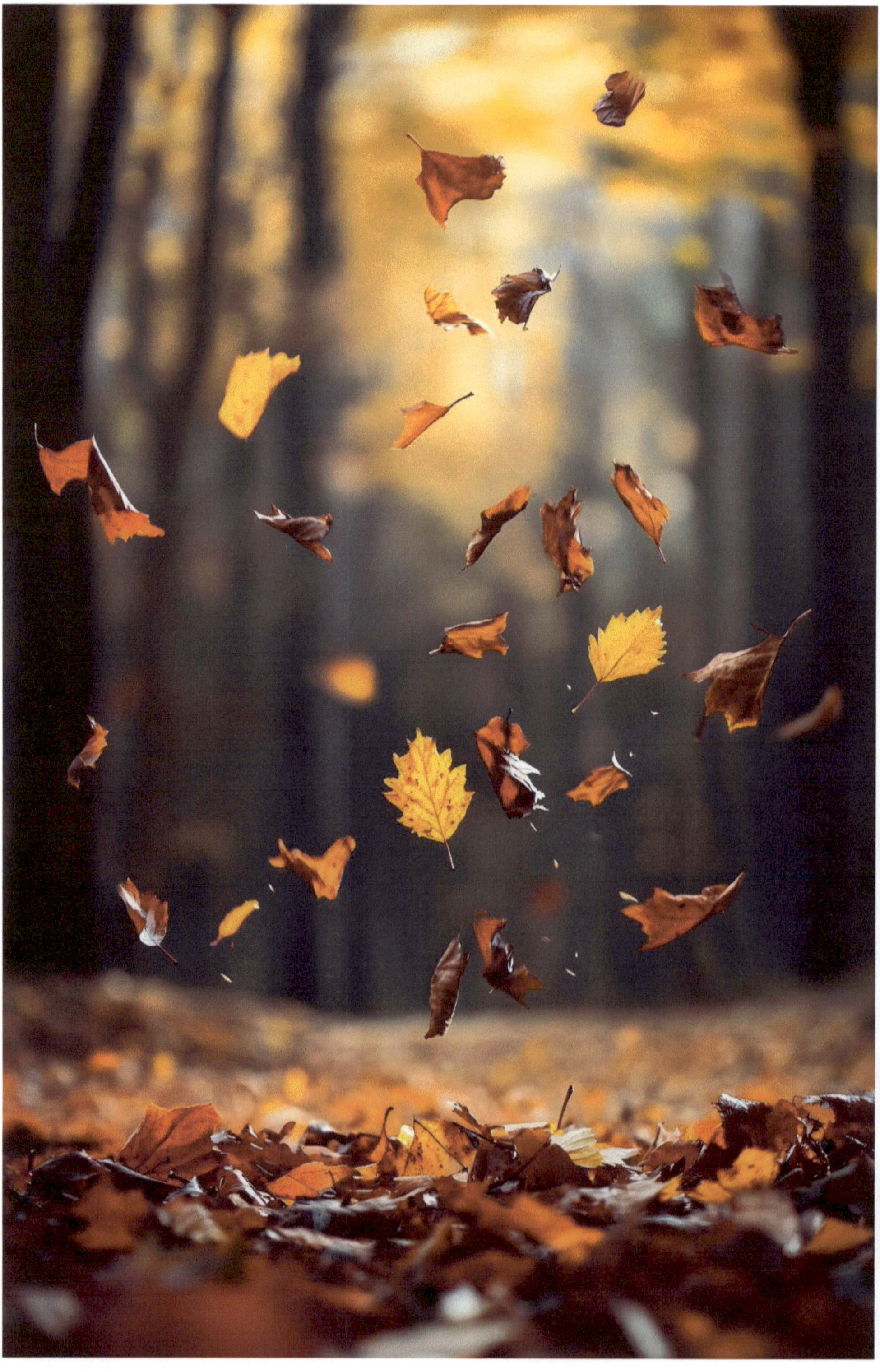

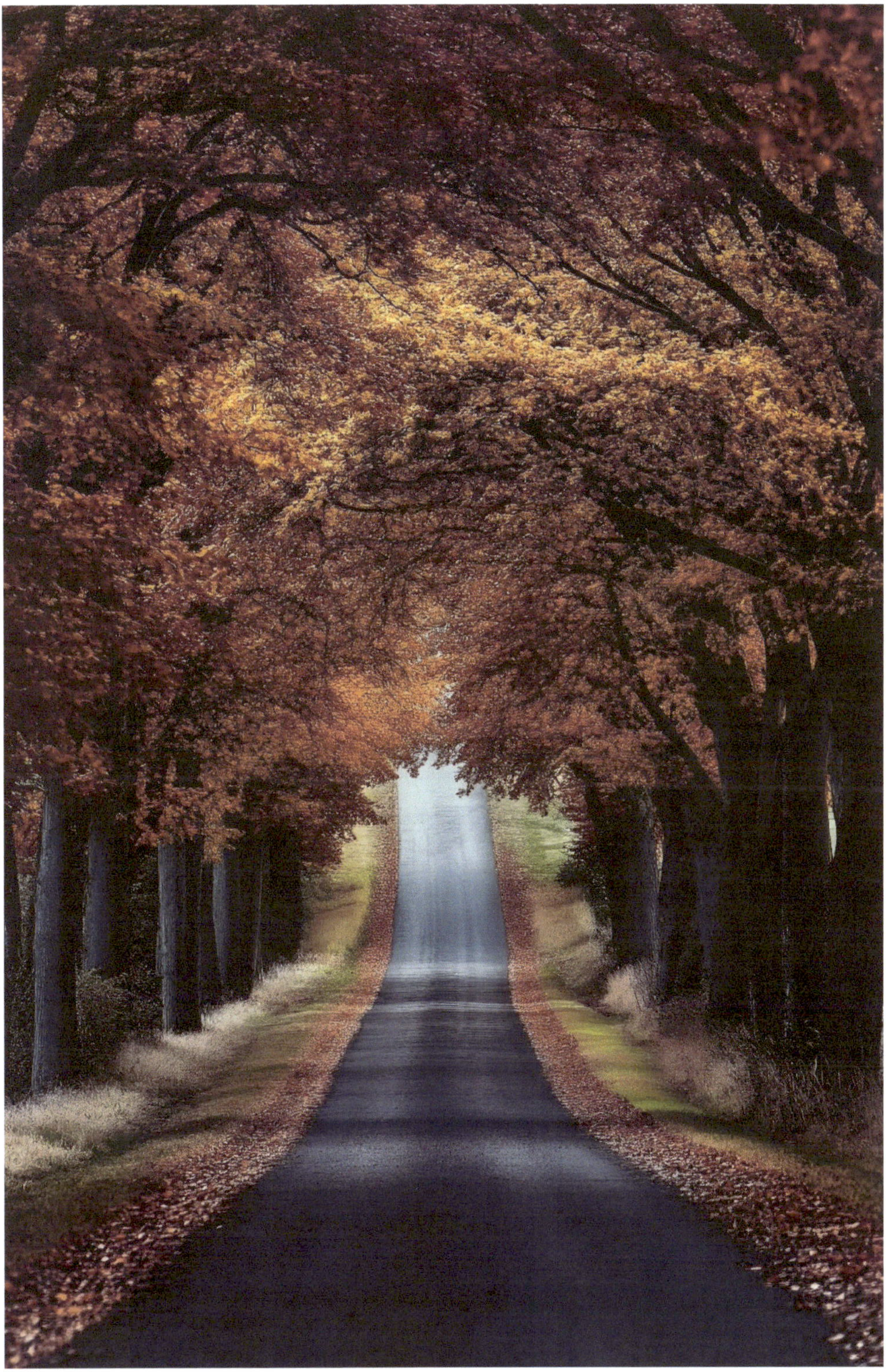

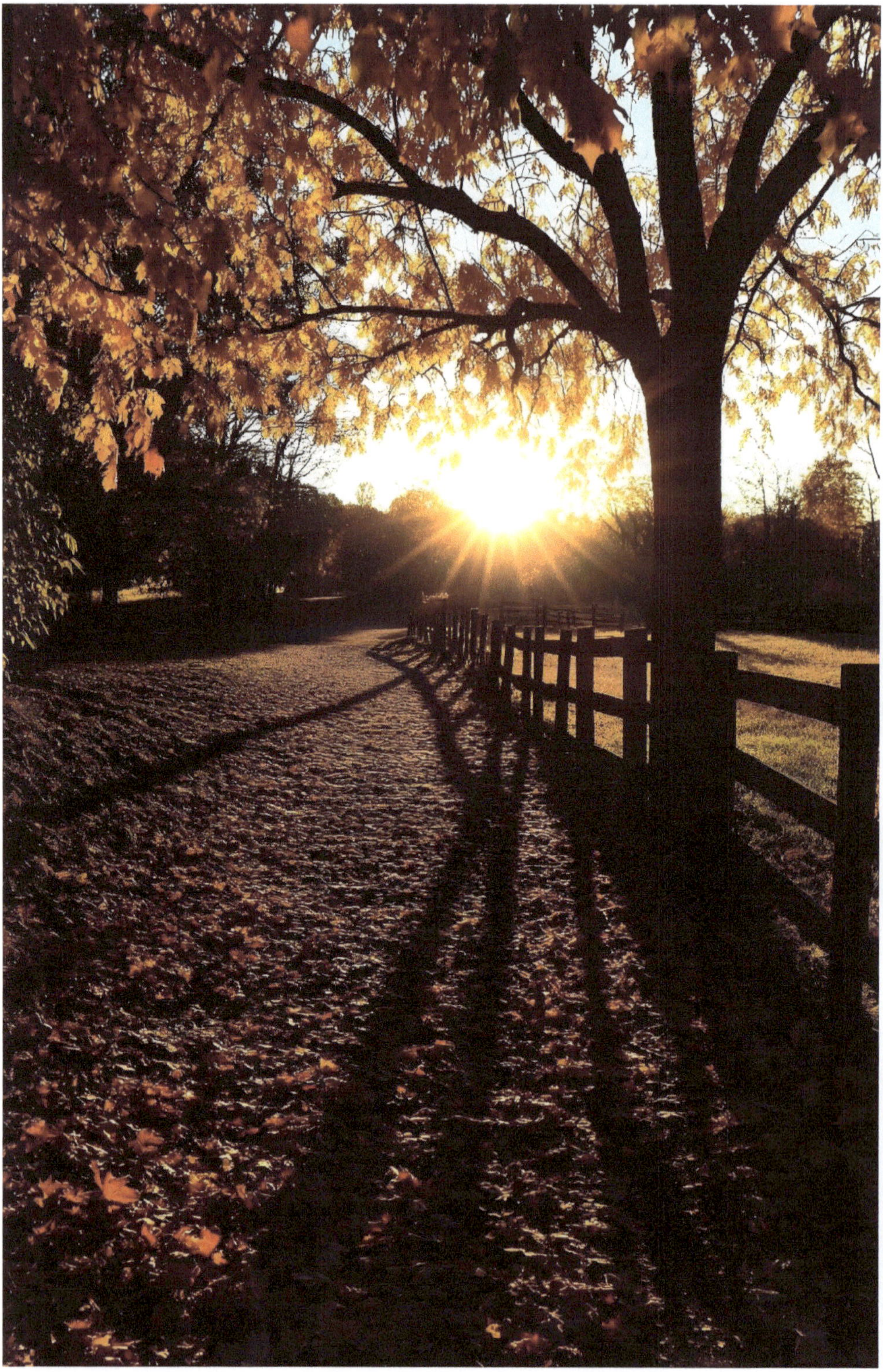

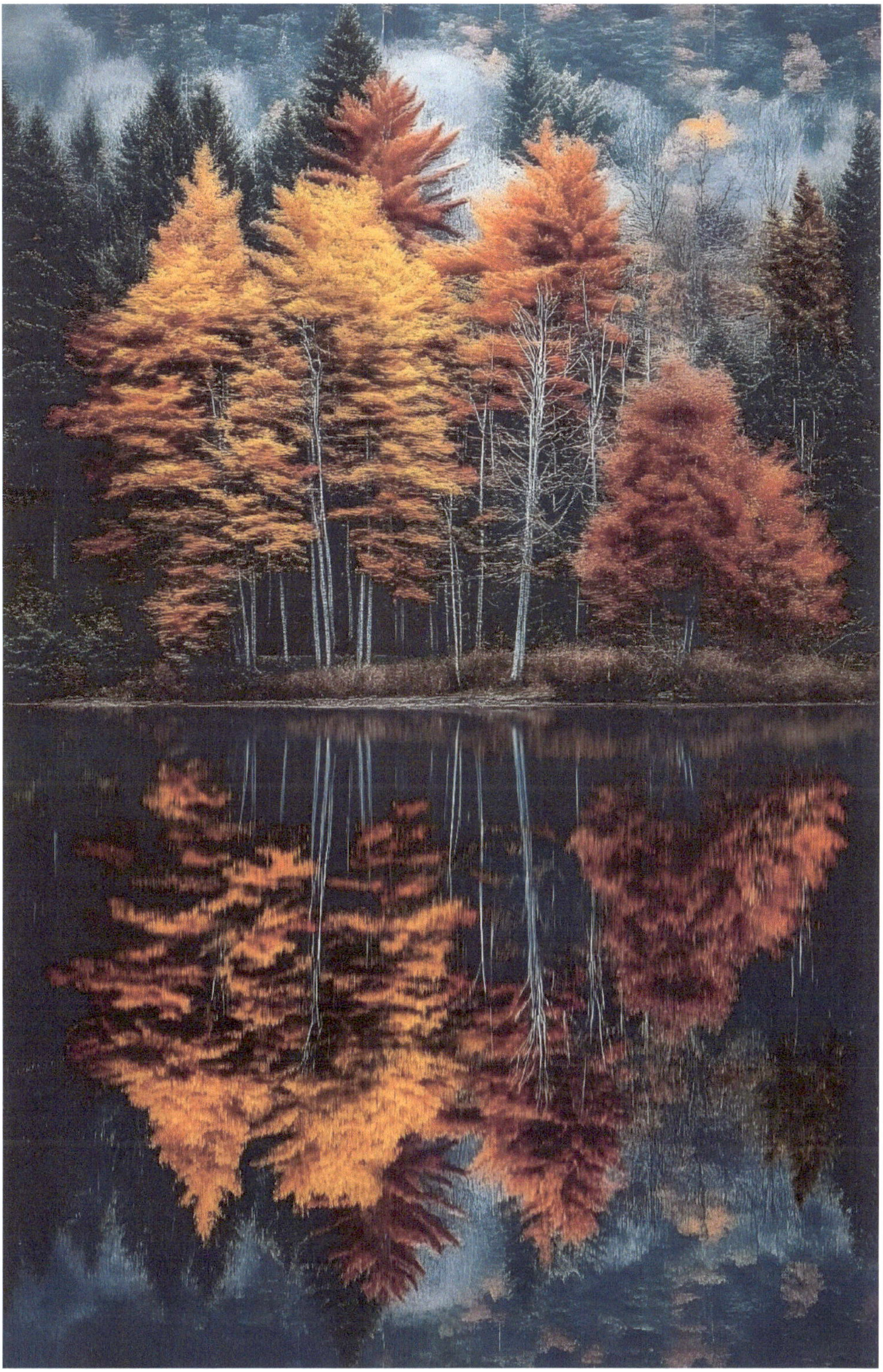

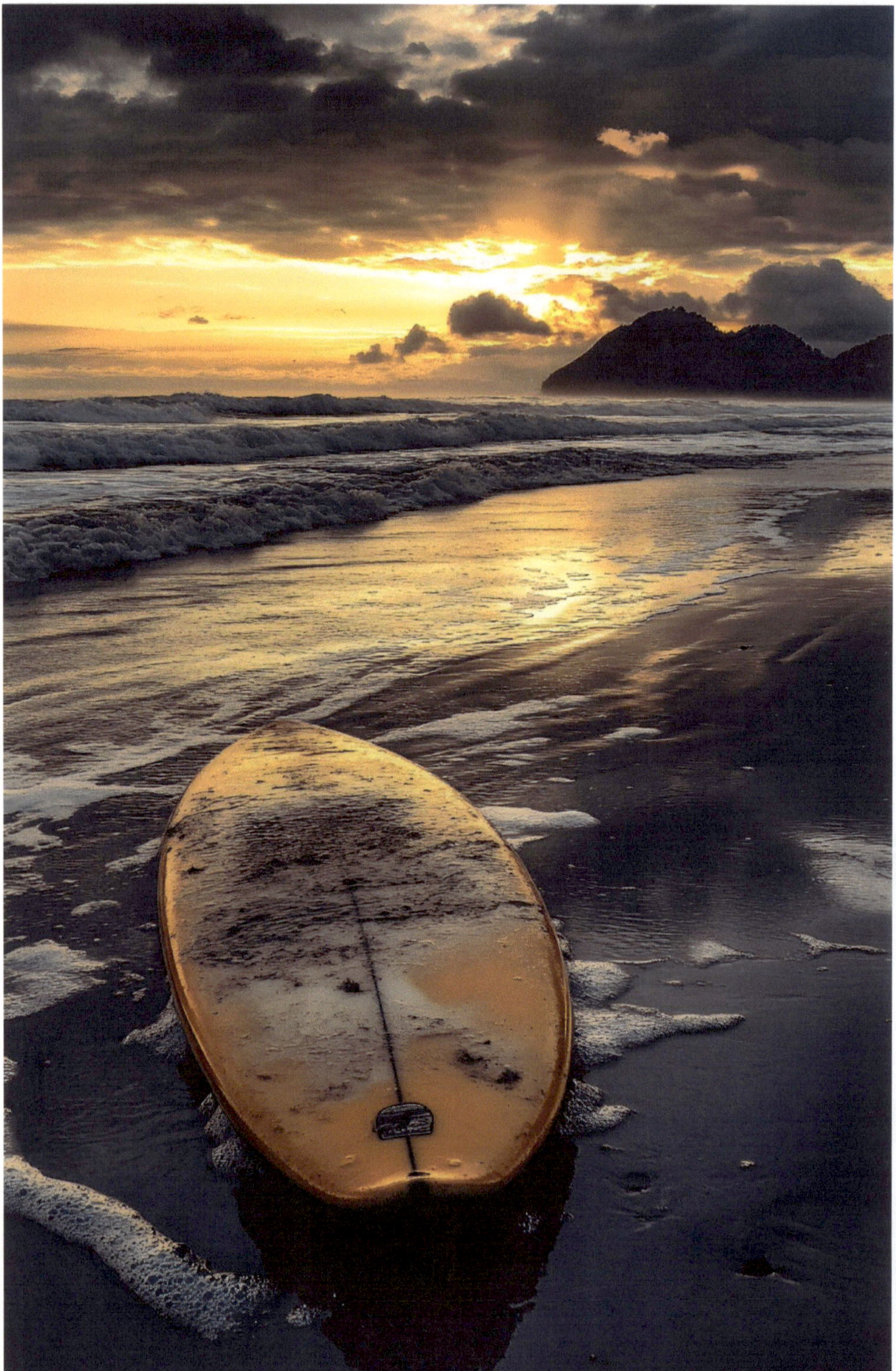

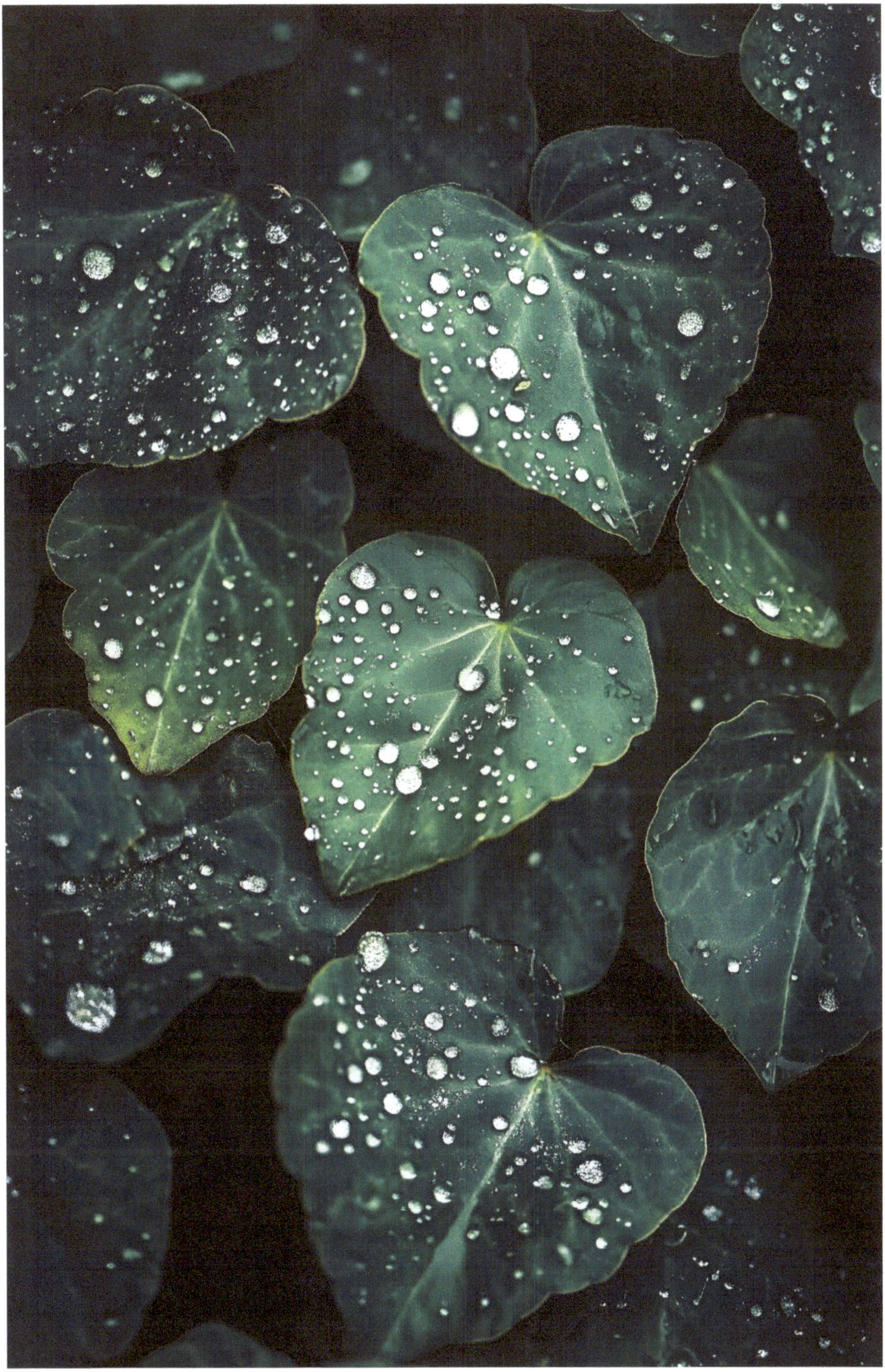

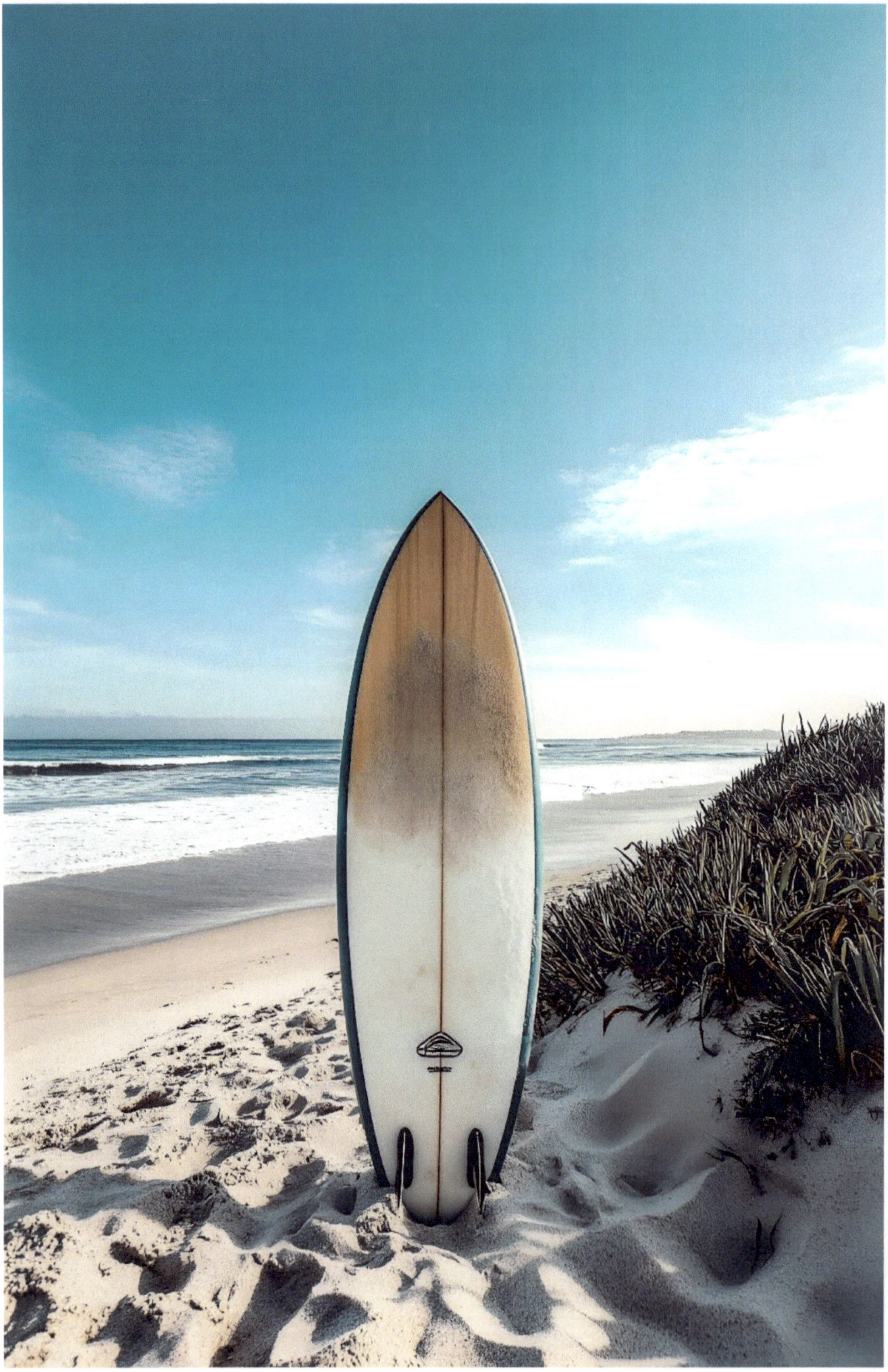

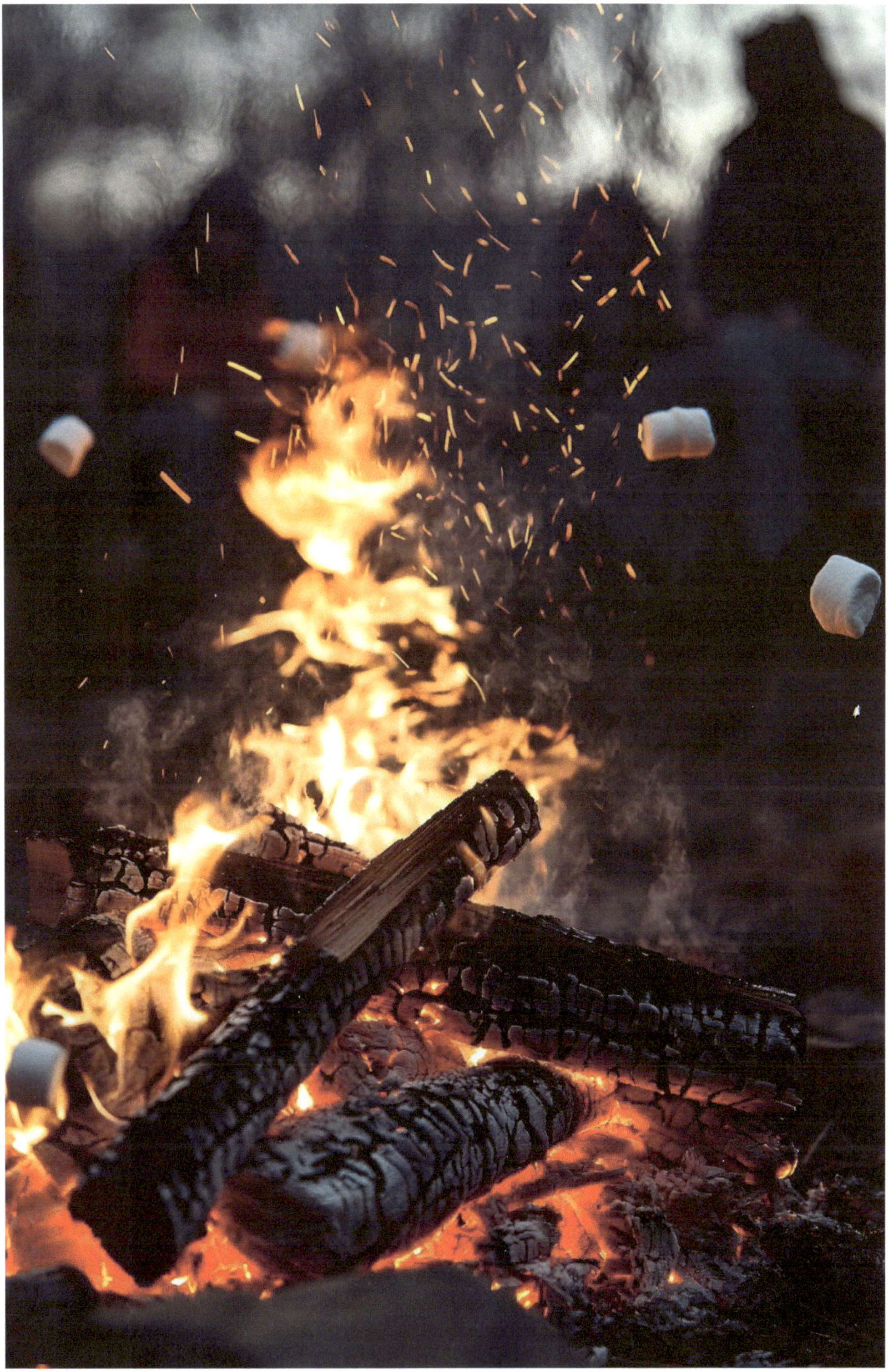

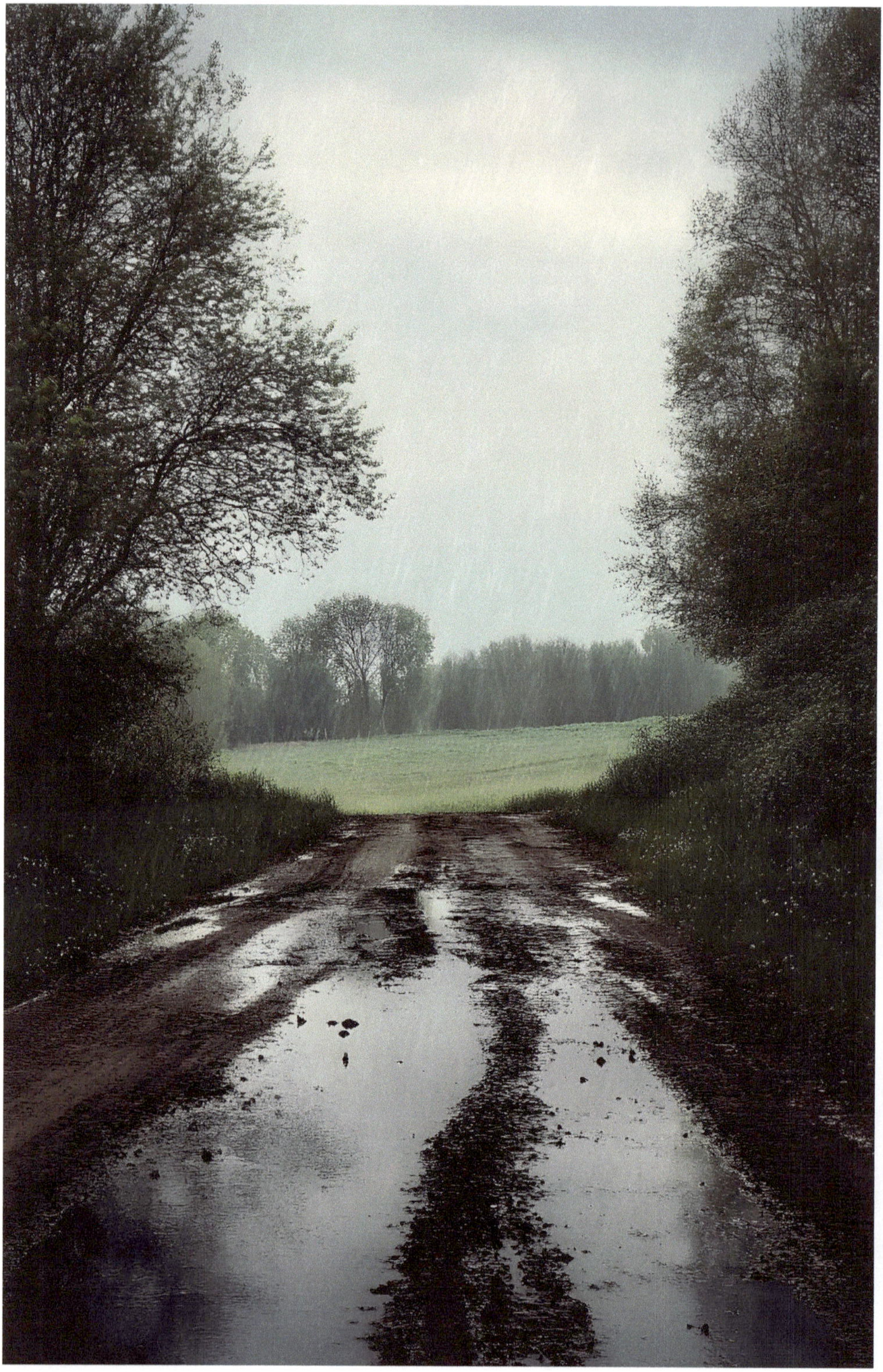

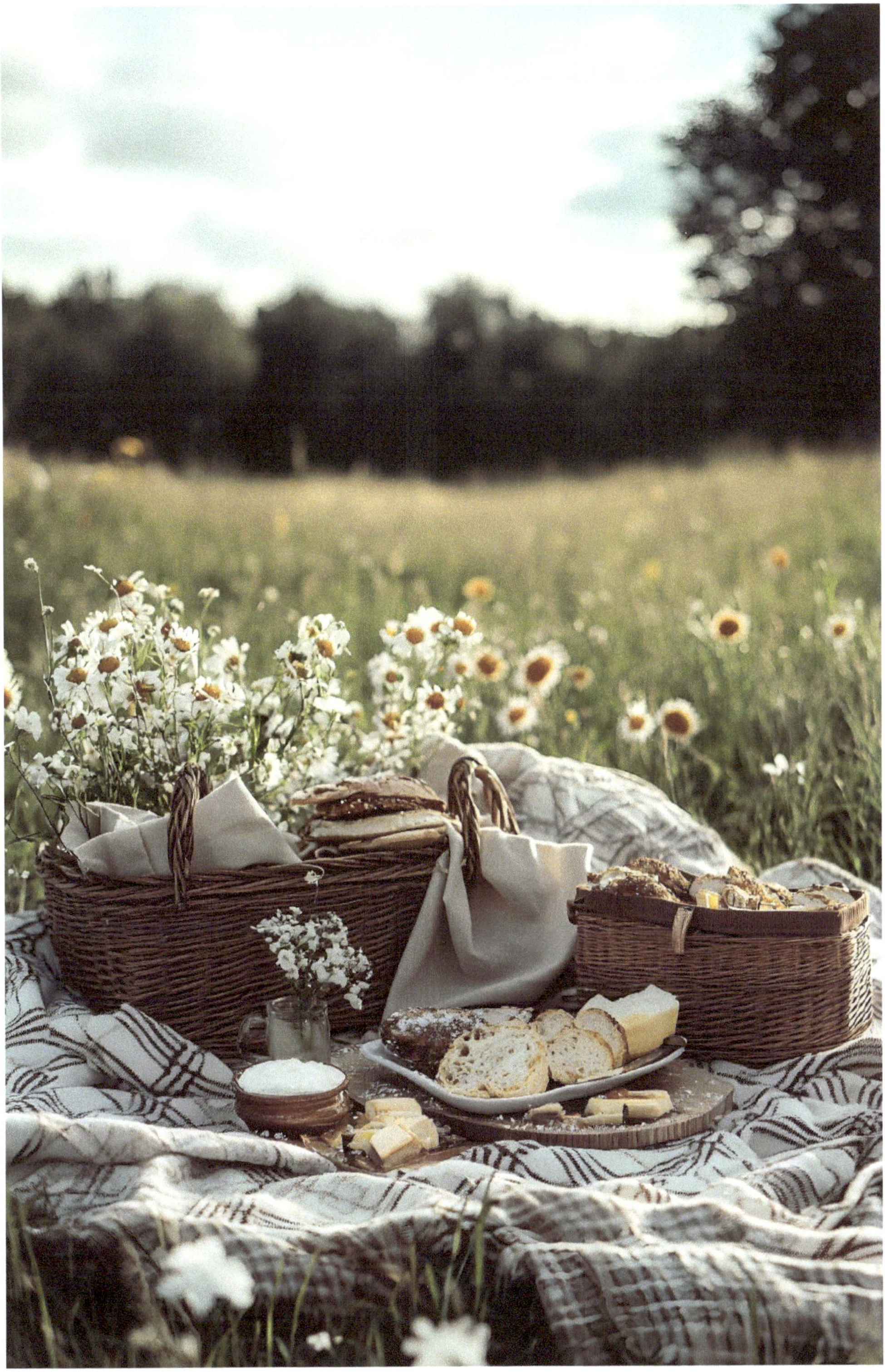

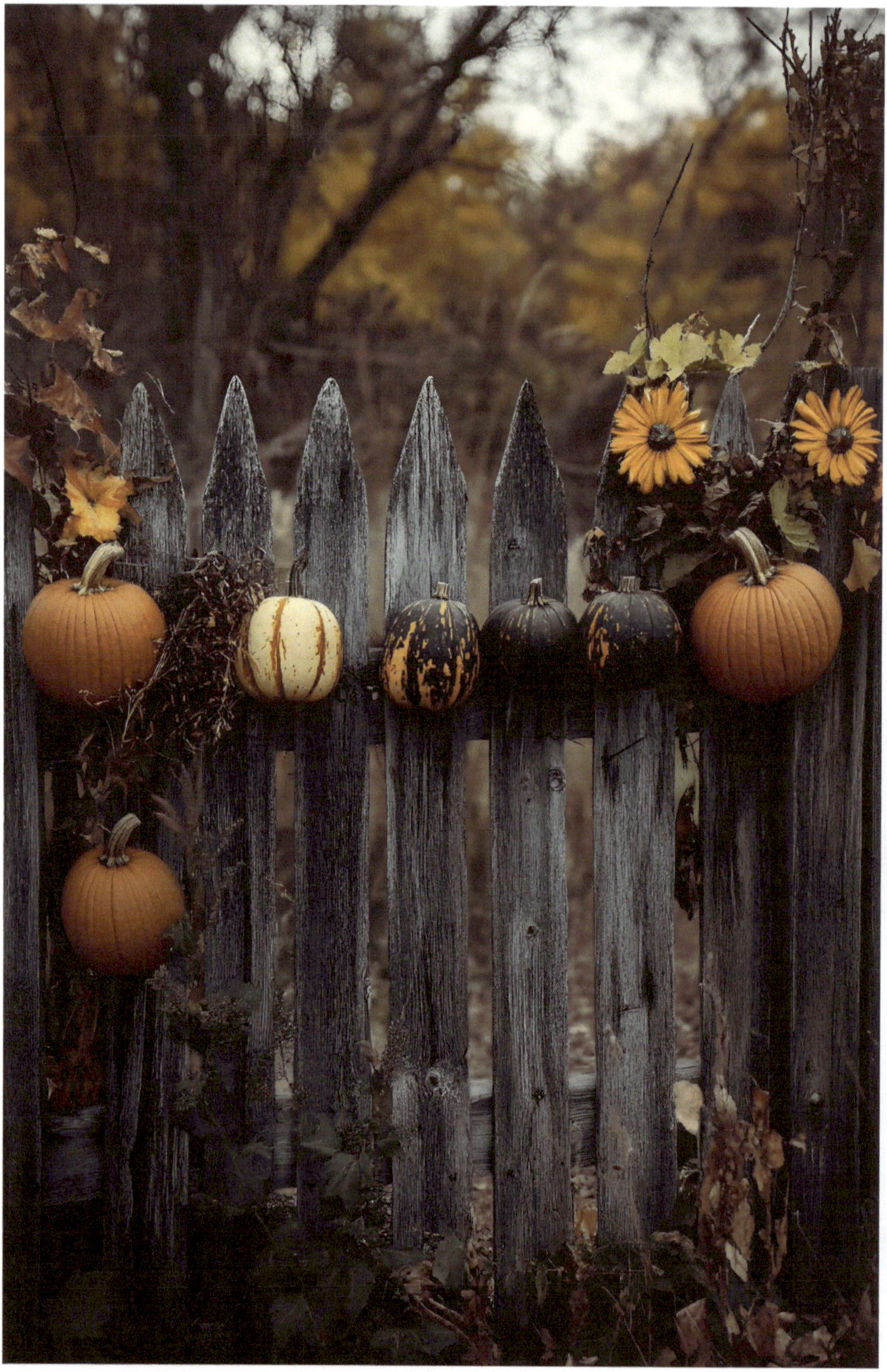

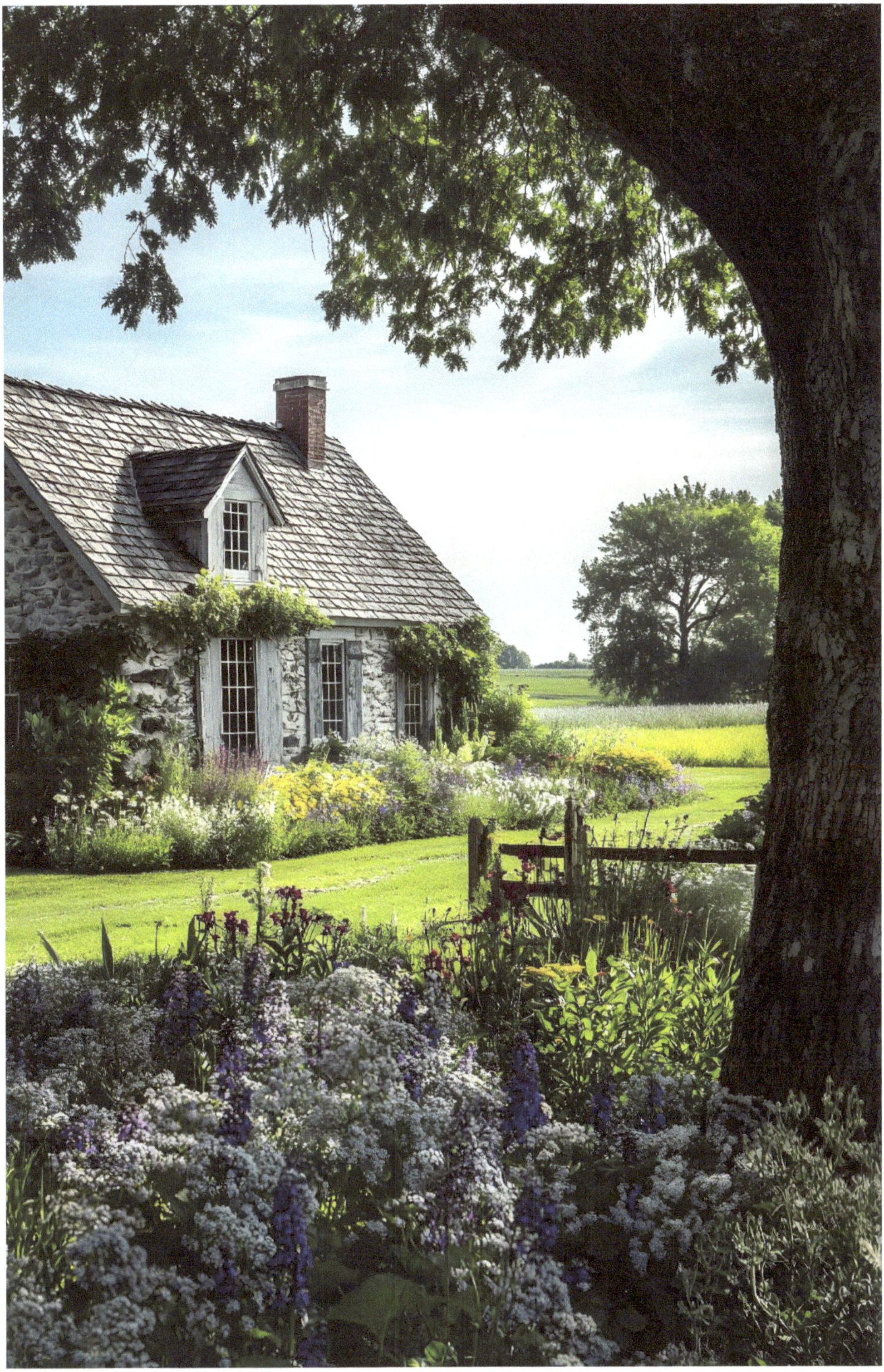

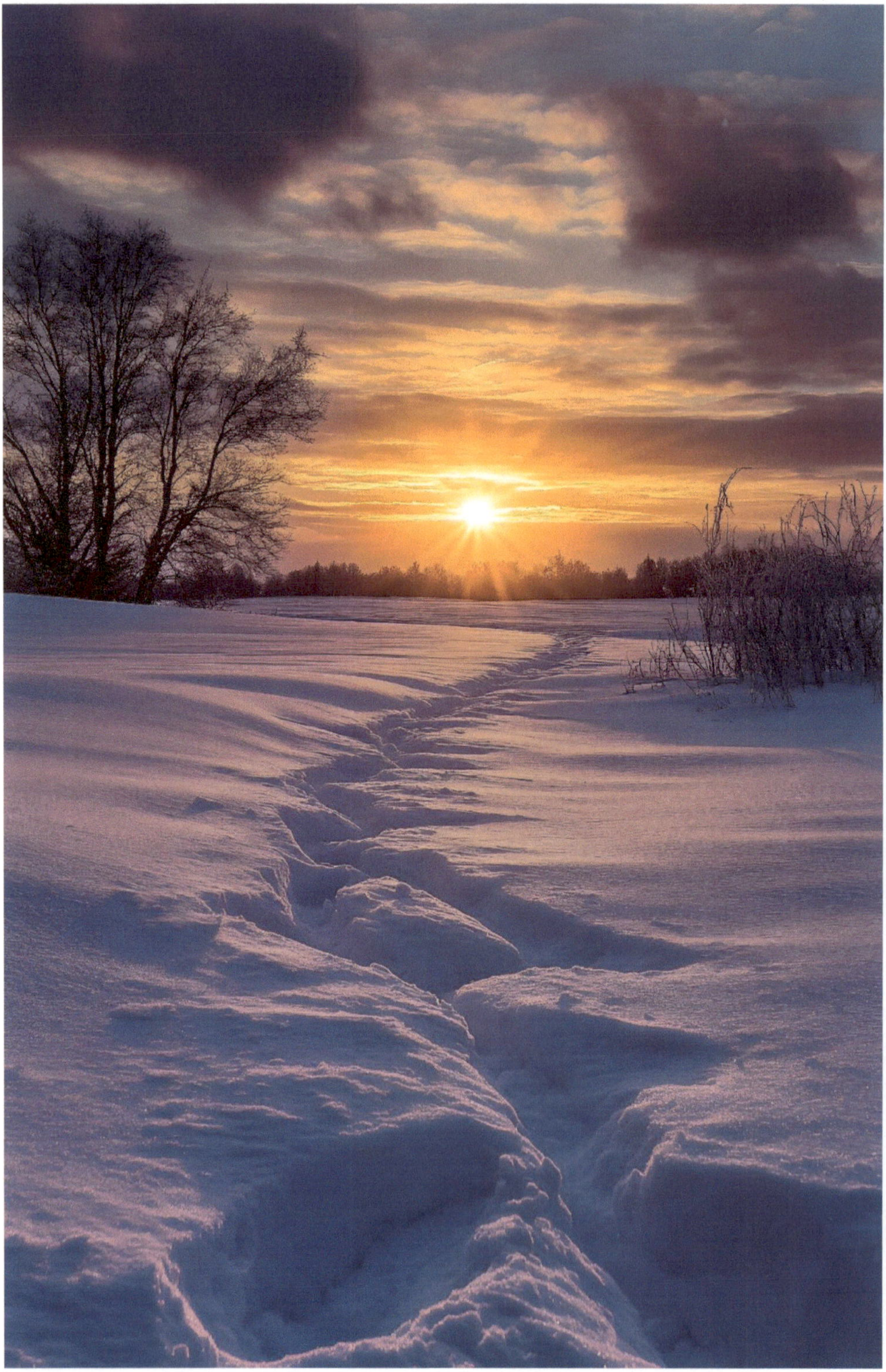

www.ingramcontent.com/pod-product-compliance
Lightning Source LLC
Chambersburg PA
CBHW040334220526
45473CB00009B/2678
9798336521627